The Dog Days of Dixon

Judy Pearson

FOUR™
PAWS
PRESS

Dixon, New Mexico

Four Paws Press
PO Box 277
Dixon, New Mexico 87527

This is a book of non-fiction. The events are real and every effort has been made to remain factually correct. Some names have been changed to protect the individual's privacy at their request or at the discretion of the author.

Book Design by happy rat studio.
For information email to DogDaysofDixon@gmail.com
www.DogDaysofDixon.com

Manufactured in the United States of America
ISBN: 978-1-7341032-0-5

This book is dedicated to all of the animal rescuers around the globe who give tirelessly to the rescue of abused, neglected, and abandoned animals. Your work is that of heroes, saints and angels.

ACKNOWLEDGMENTS

My heart is full though my brain is foggy and my body weary. The rescues in this book were in and of themselves bone-numbingly exhausting but the writing of the book was possibly my greatest challenge. There is absolutely no way it would have been completed without the help of a few near and dear. For the original nudge to write and guidance on how to get it out of my head and onto paper, I might not have done it without her encouragement; Ondrea Levine. For her brilliant editing and proofing, I owe more than I can ever repay to my friend and fellow DAPS Board member Adele Zimmermann for her detailed proofreading. She pushed when I needed it and just waited for me to make the right decision when pushing was too much. Jeannie Cornelius, our fearless leader at DAPS who supported the idea, listened to my venting and was a rational sounding board many times when I was too worked up to think or too tired to see. Violet Hill, who was an advisor and editor when I hit the tough stuff. She was intimately involved in the Albert rescue and has been a dear friend before and after the marriage. Judy Schwab, who has been my guide for decades. I would not be who I am without her teaching and insight. She has been there in the darkest of dark times as well as the lightest of days. And, along with her now departed husband, Walter, opened my consciousness to a different way of being. To all of the DAPS Board members and rescuers, today and in years past, who have all supported the work one way or another; Jennifer Birch and her daughter Leela, Jennifer Goyette, Marilyn Price-Reinbolt, Elis Wilson, Christine Kane, Cindy Ewers, Jane Lovato, Hallie and Kim Hayden and others who helped long before I arrived. The Embudo Valley is a far better place for both people and animals because of the work of all these women. And to Bob, Jeannie's husband, and Hannah, their daughter, for tolerating so many years of so many dogs! DAPS would not be what it is without your support. And to Bob personally, for keeping terminal cancer at bay for so many years. Truly remarkable that we can say "Keep calm and carry-on." And To Pat Van Kirk, who was my cheerleader since we met at the Ad Agency in 1987. The big sister I never had who was to be my editor but sadly lost her battle to cancer this past spring. Eye wheel sea ewe a gain!

"If I ever meet one of these dogs I'm going to invite him to come here, where he can be a proper dog."

Okay, I said. But remember, you can't fix everything in the world for everybody.

"However," said Ricky, "you can't do anything at all unless you begin. Haven't I heard you say that once or twice, or maybe a hundred times?"

---Mary Oliver

"Dog Songs" 2013
An excerpt from the poem "Show Time"

The Dog Days of Dixon

Table of Contents

INTRODUCTION

Dixon New Mexico is located in the northern half of the state. An hour north of Santa Fe and 30 minutes south of Taos. It is an unincorporated community governed under Rio Arriba County ordinance and law. Initially inhabited by the Tiwa people of Picuris Pueblo, it was settled in 1725 by Spanish Colonists. Numerous families that share large pieces of land that have been in the family for 400 hundred years. There are several family compounds like this in Dixon. The Spanish arrived in the area 400 years ago and many settled here to farm. Friends and neighbors, like Dana, have family that were among those settlers. The acequia system (an Arabic word for the irrigation ditches that are used by farmers across the state) was the first public works project. Dixon is the center of the Embudo Valley which includes the surrounding areas; Apodaca, Cañonicito, Rinconada, Embudo, La Bolsa, and a few others. We generally consider them all part of Dixon. This is a fertile valley and home to the highest percentage of organic farms in the state. We have two wineries and a brewery. Wine grapes have been grown in New Mexico for hundreds of years. Our local wines win national awards, and recently one of our sommeliers, Michele Padberg of the Vivac Winery, traveled throughout Europe as a guest judge in numerous international wine competitions solely representing the USA. We may be off the beaten path but there are some impressive people and institutions here.

The Vivac Winery tasting room sits on the corner of the Dixon turnoff also know as State Highway 75. It is a heavily traveled two lane road. 75 is the primary road to Penasco and points north east. It has dirt shoulders, if any at all. Everything sits on 75; the Post Office, Co-op Market, our Nationally Recognized Library, Community Centers, Elementary School (#1 in the District - again), and our New Mexico Café (owned and operated by a local family), Zuly's. There are six county roads and numerous private drives that branch off of 75 as you move through town. Homes line the highway, some sitting just feet from the shoulder. Others are set back down lengthy driveways. Four-wheel drive is a must here in inclement weather. Many homes, especially the older ones, are adobe built from local handmade clay and straw bricks. Newer homes might be straw bale or classic stick frame. Others are offset frame (stick frame with two layers of 2 x 6) so they have the look of adobe but with better insulation value. And then there are single and double wides scattered throughout the valley. So, an eclectic mix for sure.

• By the 1960s many Anglo hippies moved in as part of the Free Love Commune movement. Wavy Gravy, Lisa Law, and many others lived a few miles north in the Hog Farm Commune made famous by their involvement in the Woodstock Music Festival as both security (they renamed it The Peace Force) and a free Kitchen to feed festival-goers. Again, worth researching. You might be getting the idea by now that this little community of approximately 1500 residents if you include all of the Embudo Valley, is home to some pretty remarkable human beings. You'd be right. I don't know what the average IQ is here, but it is significantly higher than most communities, except perhaps our neighbor to the southwest, Los Alamos. Dixon has become a mix of talented, successful, educated, creative activists. Artists, writers, scientists, musicians, farmers, herbalists, curanderas (From Spain and Latin America, healers who use natural and herbal remedies.), physicians, psychologists, public servants (Politician is a tarnished word now. Those among us who run for office do so to serve.) educators, athletes, river guides, brewers and vintners (I hope I didn't miss anyone!) make up the mix here. It is an involved community that takes care of its own. The area has a rich history; I encourage you to do some research if it interests you. One event to explore is the 1951 Law Suit regarding the Separation of Church and State in schools. Dixon played a significant role. The original name El Puerto del Embudo de Nuestro Señor San

Antonio was changed around 1900 to honor Collins Dixon, a school teacher said to be a Civil War deserter. (More fascinating history to research but this isn't a history book.)

Which brings me to The Dixon Animal Protection Society (DAPS). DAPS was established when Jeannie and her husband Bob arrived here from Georgia in 1981. Jeannie was looking to start a new life after divorcing her first husband and a visit to New Mexico, with a friend and fellow potter Al Tyrell, sealed the deal. Jeannie and Bob bought an old mud-roofed adobe on the outskirts of town. Jeannie set up a pottery and Bob went to work as a builder and cabinet maker. Many homes in the area have Bob's loving touch. His work is beautiful, fine craftsmanship. Jeannie was a full-time potter and mom. At any potluck in town, you can always identify a "Jeannie pot." Her functional pottery is owned, used, and loved nation-wide. She was one of the early Dixon Studio Tour artists. (The first DST boasted 23 artists and drew 2,000 visitors! The year was 1982. It is the oldest and one of the largest Studio Tours in the state.) Soon after arriving, Jeannie learned of the enormous issue of stray and unwanted animals. In the early days, she took in 100 abandoned animals a year!

In contrast, we now see fewer than a dozen. Jeannie's 30 years of promoting and financing spay/neuter, along with educating the public on the benefits, has resulted in a sharp decline of the dumped animals in the area. In the beginning Jeannie requested donations from anyone who would listen and only adopted dogs in need of homes to those who met her strict requirements. In those early years, it was Jeannie, Adele, Hallie, Jane, and a few others she could call on in an emergency, but for all intents and purposes, she was a one-woman rescue. In 1997 DAPS received 501(c)3 non-profit status so that grants were available and donations were tax-deductible. At its peak, DAPS/Jeannie, housed 46 dogs! Plus 24 cats. After a couple of nasty dog fights, Jeannie knew something had to be done to decrease the population. A group of about 20 animal rescuers from all over northern NM met and reestablished the Española Valley Humane Society so that there was a facility for some of the abandoned animals in the county. Back then Thursday was kill day at the shelter, and thousands of animals were put down each year. The shelter is now a no-kill facility. Today they also operate a clinic for free spay/neuter to local residents, plus offer low-cost immunizations to keep animals in compliance with County ordinance and lower the risk of disease. Parvo is expensive to treat, and Distemper usually requires euthanasia, as it leaves a dog with cognitive impairment and/or behavioral and neurological issues; some become aggressive.

I arrived in June of 2011 and jumped on board as soon as the moving van was unloaded. I soon learned that things are done a bit differently here than they were back in Austin. In a large City facility, there are rules and regulations. Here, beyond the County Ordinance, which can have massive grey areas, there weren't any. We basically followed the "First do no harm" rule of healthcare workers and first responders, but beyond that, we were on our own. It was clear that I had a lot to learn about rural rescue, I was prepared for that. What I wasn't prepared for was what these rural rescues were about to teach me.

In 2012 I organized a Dog Fashion Show called "Doggie Styles." Yup, pretty cheeky. The Fashions for both dogs and humans were created by "UP-Cycled Fashions" a local upscale repurposed clothing boutique. When I spoke with them about a collaborative effort, they laughed as they had just trademarked "Pup-Cycled Fashions!" The model dogs wore outfits coordinated with those of the human models. It was delightful and a huge success. (A video should be on the website http://www.DAPSNM.org) We had hoped to make it an annual event, but life had other plans for some of us.

In February 2013 Bob was diagnosed with stage 4 pancreatic and metastatic colon cancer. He was given six weeks to live. Jeannie called to say she would not handle calls or any of the hands-on rescue work. Jeannie teaches elementary school, which takes up a lot of her time and energy. She wanted as much free time to spend with Bob as possible. I assured her I'd have it covered. Little did I know what it would entail! In May, I separated from my husband. We divorced a year later. Now six and a half years after his diagnosis, Bob is still working nearly full-time building and making cabinets. His doctors at MD Andersen don't know how or why Bob is as healthy as he is, but they suggest he keep on doing what he's doing since it's working! So, we all keep on doing what we're doing, and it is working pretty well.

As a young child I remember thinking that Dr. Doolittle was the most amazing man; and if I could just do that too! "Walk with the animals, talk with the animals, grunt and squeak and squawk with the animals and they would grunt and squeak and speak and talk to us!" I would sing that song for hours on end. Little did I know that 50 years later my community would refer to me as the dog whisperer because of the work I do with The Dixon Animal Protection Society.

I have always felt a soul connection with animals, particularly dogs and horses. I was and am allergic to cats, but I have three, all rescues. After living with them I don't have the allergic reactions I used to!

As an older child, when my sister's friend's dog had puppies I would go and have play dates, not with my sister and her friend, but with the puppies in the whelping box! I couldn't imagine anything more wonderful than sitting with a litter of puppies. The owners were always happy to have me because that meant the puppies were socialized at a very early age with someone outside the family. I had no idea I was helping, I was just in nirvana.

I had a little friend, his name was Teddy, a Lhasa Apso that lived up the street. Teddy seemed to know when I was in the yard and he would come running down the road. I was always so excited to see Teddy, what a cute sweet little dog. We would just play in the front yard, roll in the grass, do cartwheels. Of course my dad wasn't so excited because Teddy would pee on the lawn. I was in the kind of neighborhood where the manicured lawn was everyone's dream, but with our soil not so easy to achieve. But my dad worked hard keeping his beautiful lawn well manicured and green and to have a dog in the yard peeing and pooping was not appreciated. But Teddy was my friend!! Don't get me wrong, I had plenty of friends - of the human variety - who cartwheeled with me on the front lawn. But my connection to dogs has always been incredibly strong. I recognized that as a young child. I grew up in a house where pets were not allowed; no cats because we were all allergic, no dogs because, well, they peed and pooped on the lawn. And my parents, I'm sure, believed that we were too irresponsible to take care of a dog, clean up after it, take it for a walk, etc. I thought I had demonstrated otherwise but those were my parents. Two Capricorns - need I say more??

As an adult I married and bought a house; of course the first thing that yard needed was a dog. I adopted a dog in Providence from the shelter, a beautiful shepherd/husky mix who proceeded to turn the yard into a cratered landscape that made me feel like I was living on the moon. It was clear he needed a companion to keep him occupied! That next dog, Agatha, was my first experience with rescue. The dark side that sometimes has a bright side. Agatha was a boxer/lab mix, all black, beautiful dog. I adopted her on Columbus Day from the Cranston Rhode Island Shelter. She had been part of a satanic sacrifice and had been sliced open from stem to stern and left in the woods to die. Thankfully one of the kids involved got scared and called the police; told them where they would find her. They found her alive and rushed her to the vet who closed her up and treated her infection. When she was healed enough she was put up for adoption. Her labia never did heal. We tried a second surgery but it just would not take so she always peed a little sideways.

I almost named her Zipper since the staples down her belly looked like a zipper. I didn't. I called her Agatha, after Agatha Christie, because it was a mystery how she survived. Her story could easily have been one of murder. The minute I met her I knew she was my dog.

I divorced my husband and went to graduate school. I earned a Masters degree in ceramics, and Agatha accompanied me to the studio because I often worked late, alone. The security guards were very pleased that I had her with me. She was an alpha and very protective but she was also very sweet. They started keeping dog biscuits in their pockets because she would be defensive, but offer her a treat and everything was fine. She died just before turning 15, of old age; she was a wonderful dog. And a soulmate or spirit dog.

I have read a number of books lately on following your soul path, soul work, and soul vibration. They speak of our energy vibrations - whether we're human, plant, or animal; we all have a particular frequency. It is said that animals' vibrations are at a higher frequency. That higher vibration is often equated with having reincarnated or recycled many times and all of our karmic lessons have been learned. I find this a very interesting concept in many ways. I have often said I wanted to reincarnate as my own dog. I don't think that's possible but I always liked the idea because I know my dogs will be well loved and well treated and, since many of them are victims of abuse, abandoned or feral, they are the ones who feel safe with me. This deep soul connection and the comfort of frightened, abused, shy dogs with me is something for which I've never had the words to describe or explain until now. I have often called it love, a pure love that connects but that didn't feel complete. I now believe it is a vibrational frequency that makes these dogs feel comfortable and makes me feel so deeply connected. That could also be a love vibration so perhaps both. And it is not just me!! The internet is flooded with videos of dogs rescued from near death having been starved, dumped, or abused into a state of shutdown yet when they are reunited with their rescuer they are full of love and excitement! They feel the connection deeply enough to want to live and usually end up adopted by the rescuer who shares the deep connection. They don't respond to other people in the same way. I do believe those who will stop to rescue these poor creatures are on a higher vibration themselves. And the animals know it! I know some of you will think that anyone would rescue an animal. I can assure you that is not the case. I have now come to believe that these people are at a lower vibrational frequency. They have either not done their soul work to raise their vibrations or they have not reincarnated many times and are just "new." There is no judgment associated with lower vibration. It is not good or bad it just is. This idea may not resonate with you and that is okay too. For me it answers questions I have pondered since childhood.

A number of years before Agatha died I met the man who would become my second husband; he lived in Austin, Texas. Once I moved to Austin I continued to rescue dogs and with hurricane Katrina in 2005, I became heavily involved with animal rescue effort. A friend of mine was organizing the volunteers and volunteer veterinarians with the Austin Humane Society where the animals were being housed when people bussed in from New Orleans to Austin to escape the hurricane. This was the beginning of my dog whisperer career. We had a tiny little long-haired Yorkie-Poo come in. He was so petrified, shutdown, absolutely filthy and boy did he smell bad. No one could get him out of his crate. Because I'm not very big, I'm only 5' 3" and an athlete, I could crawl into his crate and within minutes he was in my lap happily licking my face. From there we went to the clinic and he had a bath and we went outside and sat in the sun to dry, he was so very cute. I was not a small dog lover by any means but that little guy pulled at my heartstrings no question. A few weeks later I asked what had happened with him. His owner unfortunately had lost her house, she had nothing but a concrete slab and had to start over. She was overwhelmed. She didn't know what she was going to do so she released him to the Austin Humane Society to find a new home. I adopted him. His name was Midnight. I kept the name; it suited him, and I didn't think he needed to face another change. My husband wasn't exactly thrilled to have another dog but the connection was too strong to deny this little guy. He lived with me until four years ago when he died suddenly of a mystery illness that may have been caused by exposure during the hurricane. Many of the animals that were rescued have since developed aggressive cancers and passed away. But the hurricane rescue effort was the impetus to become a regular volunteer with the Austin Humane Society. I quickly moved up through the ASPCA training program as a dog walker, trainer, shy dog handler, and photographer for the Austin Humane Society for seven years until we moved to New Mexico in 2011. And that is when the real adventures began. Here are those first stories....

A Little Bit Of Sunshine
by Juan Olivarez

A little bit of sunshine every day,
Helps to keep the rain clouds far away.
A little bit of sunshine, for your soul,
Helps you to weather even bitter cold....

Photo by Judy Pearson

Sunshine

Sunshine was my first Dixon Animal Protection Society (DAPS) Rescue. I can't say that I was prepared for this, but it needed to happen. This rescue was to be a baptism by fire both figuratively and literally! It was in late winter 2012. I had only been with DAPS for about seven months when my first call to rescue came in.

There was concern for this dog because it was unusually cold. We get snow, but the average daytime temps are in the 30s. The sun is strong here so winter days are generally quite beautiful. At the time we were in the single digits during the day and below zero at night. Septic systems and water lines were freezing. There were outages all over the region. Thousands of homes were without heat and water. We had never experienced anything like this here. People were suffering; a few didn't survive. It wasn't the freezing temperatures that left Danny's home without heat, though. The house had burned the week before. The garage was full of empty oil cans, cans of paint, and other combustibles. It was only a matter of time before there was going to be a fire.

"You have to do something about the dog!" I heard this several times during the week. My response was the same each time, "What dog?!" I admit I was getting a bit annoyed. And, I was starting to understand that anyone who had lived here for any length of time assumed everyone knew everyone, their dog(s), and where they lived. I had been introduced to a whole bunch of folks, having lived here only for a short time, but there were many more I had yet to meet, dogs too. I also understood that since Jeannie knew the people concerned, by association, I should too! That just wasn't the case, and now, eight years later, it still isn't! Jeannie knows locals I have never met and I know others she never has. We run in slightly different social circles that overlap quite a bit but, on a day-to-day basis, we interact with very different factions of the community.

One afternoon I went to the Co-op for a few groceries; once again, I was told, by the cashier, that I had to do something about "the dog." This had happened twice in a row now. Two different cashiers on different days said precisely the same thing. The second time it was Kim Hayden. I knew a little about Kim but didn't know her well, yet. We would get to know each other over time as she became my pet sitter when my husband and I traveled. Kim and her mother Hallie had been long-time animal rescuers for DAPS. Working cashier meant Kim met everyone who lived here, anyone who visited, or was just passing through. She'd have the inside scoop for sure, so finally, I might get to the bottom of this dog thing! I had a strange feeling about this particular rescue. Was it just that I was new? I didn't think so. Something was odd, and it would take a little time to know what but it felt like I was being set up. People had been calling the Co-op trying to find me to "do something." Some of these folks lived right next door to the dog in question, so I was a bit concerned as to why they hadn't done anything.

I asked Kim, "This dog I keep hearing about, do you know what dog people are talking about?" She told me, "Well, it's the dog in the burned-out house, Danny's dog." I still didn't have a clue! I didn't know Danny, and I knew nothing about a burned-out house. It seemed that everyone thought I knew about the dog and Danny.

I had heard a little about him, and from that, I knew I didn't want to actually know the man. Admittedly, I had assumed that, with this being such a small community, news and gossip would spread like the fire in Danny's house. But it didn't. In some ways, that was reassuring. I'd heard stories from friends who lived in gossipy small towns where everyone's business was everyone else's business. Clearly, I had to get in the loop to be better informed. Kim was part of the inner circle, and so she filled me in on Danny. He was a local drug addict.

I actually had met Danny, but he used the name, Michael. Shortly after we moved in "Michael" had come to the house looking for money to pay for his daughter's funeral in Albuquerque. He said she had died of cancer. It sounded disingenuous to me, and I did not give him any money, but he had gotten to my husband before I did, and he was now out twenty bucks. I guess Danny/Michael was convincing. It seems he was surprisingly fast to hit up the new residents who had not yet learned of his history. That was my first hint as to who he was . I knew we would not be friends.

Now with the information I had been missing, it was clear that we needed to get to "the dog" as soon as possible. No dog was going to survive very long in these frigid temperatures, particularly in a house with no roof, let alone no heat. Kim asked to be let off work early so we could go get "the dog" before it had to suffer another frigid night alone. This is one of the beautiful things I was finding out about this community, it is a real community.

Kim is about 5'8" and a substantial woman. She'd been in a severe car accident and was still dealing with pain from the multiple injuries. Walking was a chore. She walked as much as she could, but it was difficult and often painful. Kim is from Kentucky and has a "take no prisoners" approach to just about everything. She doesn't take BS from anyone, and she is no dummy. She has a quick mind and an even sharper wit. I liked her immediately! I remember asking what part of Texas she was from. I thought she would choke me to death. The look she gave was bone-chilling, Then she cracked a smile and told me to never say that ever again or she would have to kill me. Seems she really didn't like Texans. She is a *Kentucky* girl, and I never would forget it. That established, we took a drive down the road. It wasn't more than about a mile from the Co-op that we turned down the long dirt driveway to Danny's house. I was thrilled that she knew where it was because it was almost impossible to see from the highway, and I would have wasted a whole lot of time searching for it. The driveway was rutted and dotted with dead grass. It obviously wasn't seeing a whole lot of traffic these days. Danny no longer had a car.

The house was an older adobe sitting out on a little plateau. It didn't look very safe. The plateau wasn't a whole lot wider than the house. Just feet from the house it dropped about 25 feet, nearly straight down, to the fields below. I wondered how much erosion had occurred since the house was built and how much time before it would just slide down as the ground continued to give way. I had never seen this house. There are lots of homes like this around Dixon, off the main road, kind of hidden from view. To the left of the house was a tree under which I thought we'd see the dog tied. No dog.

We did a quick look around and saw that most of the roof was indeed gone. What was left was a blackened spine with charred ribs. Only the far west end of the living room and the room beyond had any roof left at all. The rest was wide open to the frigid sky. What used to be the garage was a gaping black cavern. Piles of burned cans stood in the corner, there had to be hundreds of them. It was remarkable that there was anything left of the house at all. What was left smelled of the recent blaze. I like the smell of fire, but this was different, acrid and damp. It gave me chills.

Kim and I peered in a window to see what exactly "the dog" might look like. After hearing about Danny, I figured he owned a pit bull. Before I go on, I am not anti-pit bull. I have known some very sweet, loyal pitties and in general, like the breed. But it did cross my mind that Danny might want a watchdog for protection and pits are very popular around these parts. But I couldn't have been more wrong! As I looked in the window, there, sitting on the sofa, was a little Chihuahua mix. A chubby little sausage dog. We call them Chiweenies; half Chihuahua and half dachshund. She was shaking hard, her eyes bulging with fear and/or cold. Scooping up a scared aggressive Chihuahua was not high on my list of fun. Still, this little golden 20-pound chi mix could not be left in this house! The structure was so badly damaged it looked like it might fall in at any moment and the wind was picking up! I had visions of being pinned under the falling trusses as I grabbed this little dog. Time was of the essence, so I tried the front door; it was locked. I gave it a shove thinking it might just be stuck. It wasn't, my shoulder would vouch! I tried turning the knob again with more force, nothing. I considered going in through the burned-out garage, but that seemed too risky. On any dog rescue, my first priority is keeping the people safe, including me. I hoped there was another way in. I kept looking over my shoulder to be sure Danny wasn't coming down the driveway. My breathing was heavy though I wasn't really exerting myself, and my heart was pounding. The dog wasn't the only scared one. Kim seemed a little nervous as well. She knew Danny and had said she wasn't too keen on running into him. She knew he had a history of fighting. We had heard that Danny was in the hospital.

I had a strong sense that someone was watching. I was pretty sure it was the neighbors that tipped us off to the dog being abandoned. More likely than not, they were glad the dog was being removed from the house and, that it wasn't them doing it! Even if they saw us when Danny returned they would swear they knew nothing, saw nothing; we didn't have to ask for that. If they did give us up, Jeannie is one of the people Danny was afraid of so we were good either way. He wouldn't dare cross her. Let me give you a quick description of Jeannie, she's a Little Firecracker. She's five feet tall, blonde, and as of this writing just turned 72 years old. You would never know it though. She looks at least ten years younger.

She is not physically imposing (nor am I), but she knows him. She'd just tell it like it is and he'd have nothing left to say. She'd deliver it with the fury of an animal activist who has seen it all one too many times.

I left Kim out front to stand guard and went around the house looking for open windows, a back door, any ingress I could find that meant I wasn't going to have to break in to get into the house. I'll do a lot for a suffering animal, but breaking and entering wasn't a consideration. Danny supposedly had a friend feeding the dog, so if necessary, we might be able to get a key from her. I thought again about the garage. The garage was mostly gone and the roof, or what was left of it, was pretty unstable. Even rattling the door was just too dangerous. So I came back to the front to tell Kim I couldn't find a way to get in. I wasn't looking at her; I was still scanning the house. When I looked up, there she stood with the front door wide-open. I was flabbergasted! "How did you get it open?" I asked. "I turned the knob." she said. "What? I turned the knob, and it didn't budge! I was sure it was locked!" I exclaimed incredulously. She said, "Well, I must've turned it the other way." Rather than stand there and waste time puzzling over why I couldn't open the front door, I laughed, feeling like an idiot, and we went in. At least the laugh had broken the tension, a bit.

Not knowing this dog, and still unsure of how she was going to react to our presence, I approached with extreme caution. Yes, she was small, but Chihuahuas could be vicious! I wished I had thrown a blanket in the car, I could wrap her up and protect myself. We looked in the bedroom for a blanket or sheet, but everything was covered in burned ceiling debris. I didn't have time to search any further, so I was just going to have to face this little dog. As I got closer and looked at her face, it was quite clear the poor thing was just frightened and suffering from hypothermia. She was wedged between the sofa cushions looking a bit like a hot dog in a bun. I approached her slowly; she showed no signs of aggression. Her big brown, almost black, eyes were soft and friendly. I picked her up and stuffed her in my coat to warm her up. When she licked my cold nose, I knew we were going to be OK! I had to choke back tears thinking about how long she had been left alone in this freezing roofless house without heat or food. How many days? There were feces and urine covering the living room carpet, so it had clearly been a while. There were cheap paper plates strewn about that showed evidence that they had, at some point, had dog food on them, but there was now no food in sight, only a bowl of water which had frozen into a block of ice.

We looked around the sparsely furnished room; a stained and sagging matching sofa set that had seen far better days, a small particle board bookshelf displaying a couple of awards and photos of the kids, and a small TV stand with an outdated television lined the room. To the right was the bedroom; closest to the garage. I was surprised it wasn't burned worse than it was. It appeared that the fire crossed the house in the roof and ceiling east to west. On the other side was the kitchen. At one time this was probably a comfortable home. Not anymore.

Kim went in the kitchen to poke around and learn a little more about Danny based on his food choices. There were empty dog food cans in the sink, so clearly someone had been in to feed her but when? It looked like she hadn't eaten for a few days at best.

I didn't want to spend another second in this creepy place. To say it smelled is an understatement; an acrid combination of wet charred wood, motor oil, and dog excrement. And it was cold! The wind blew, and the ceiling creaked and swayed. Something fell on the bed. Kim and I looked at the ceiling and then at each other, eyes wide, sharing the thought that the remainder of the roof could come down at any second. I didn't have to say a word. We turned and bolted for the door. The dog was nestled under my chin to protect her from any falling debris. We jumped in the car and drove out, oh so grateful to have not met Danny that evening!

Who could do this to such a sweet, sweet little dog? Or any dog. Abandon her in a roofless house with no heat, in extreme cold, no food, no comfort, and no idea when someone would come get her. I still wasn't sure how she survived the sub zero nights. Kim held the dog while I drove, so now it was her turn for sweet kisses of gratitude. This dog was just adorable. We both petted and talked to her all the way to Kim's house. I dropped Kim at home, though she didn't want to put the dog down, and I headed to my place with her on my lap, snuggled into my warmth. I couldn't wait to introduce this little girl to my pack. I had no idea how she would interact with the other dogs. She seemed so sweet; I hoped it would be OK.

After warming and feeding my new friend, I gave her a quick exam to see if there were any immediate medical concerns. That's when I noticed her paws. When we went into the house to get her, she was snuggled down into the cushions of the sofa. Smart girl, that probably kept her from freezing to death, but I wondered why she hadn't jumped off the couch when we entered. I could now see why, her toenails circled a complete 360°!! They hadn't been trimmed in years! She wasn't able to walk, never mind jump off a sofa. A closer look revealed that at least one of them had grown back into the toe pad. I was horrified and disgusted. This was nothing short of abuse!

We often speak of neglect and abuse in animal rescue and the terms can be a bit vague and used interchangeably. To me neglect does not infer an immediate threat to life and limb. It may be unkind or uncomfortable but not immediately threatening. An example might be not feeding an animal for a short time. A few days without is not nice, but it will not mean the demise of the animal. Long-term neglect, such as starving an animal for an extended period then crosses the line into abuse as it *does* threaten the life of the animal. For me the other defining factor is pain. If it causes immediate pain, injury or death, I see it as abuse. Again it can be vague and there are grey areas. Allowing this little dog's nails to grow too long is neglect. Allowing them to grow back into her paw pads, where they then cause immediate pain, is abuse.

It took some time; she was not used to, nor comfortable with, having her nails trimmed. Many dogs dislike it, but I was able to trim the toenails short enough for her to walk. I'd cut them again in a few days. The quick needed time to recede. The quick is the vein in the center of the claw or nail. It isn't very large but if cut it bleeds profusely. The quick grows and recedes with the length of the nail. I didn't want to trim them back all at once and cause bleeding. Once they start flowing, it is hard to stop. She wouldn't bleed to death, but I didn't want to cause her any more trauma. For now, they were short enough for her to get around comfortably.

She was now ready to meet my gang. They were all curious, and she just sat calmly as each dog sniffed and introduced themselves. She was totally non-dog-reactive, woot-woot! What a huge relief. Curiously she was also not interactive. She had been an only dog and may have preferred it that way. The next morning I took her to the vet to get her shots and a full examination. Generally, she was in good health, and everyone at the clinic adored her. I named her Sunshine because her disposition is so sunny, and she is the color of the warm light at the end of the day, a deep golden yellow-tan. She has the sweetest little white face with those big dark eyes. It soon became apparent that it is the perfect name. When I let her out in the dog yard, she loves to sit in the sunshine! She turns her little face, eyes just slits, up to face the warm sun and I swear she is smiling!

It seemed odd that the neighbors didn't go in and get the dog if they knew she had been left alone. They knew she was sweet and petite, so why didn't they? I got that answer when I ran into one of the people who had called to ask me to rescue the dog. I asked, "Why didn't you go in and get the dog?" "Because Danny is dangerous!" they replied. OH KAY thanks for letting me know! I said I had felt like I was being set up and there it was. I am actually glad I didn't know then what I know now! Had I known I would have called animal control for assistance and not taken this on. I was delighted to hear that Danny would be in the hospital for a few more days! Yes, I could have called animal control to handle this, but we are in rural New Mexico, and we have one, yup, one, Animal Control officer for the entire county. And it is a BIG County. He is good, outstanding even, but we only call him in when truly necessary. Like when we have aggressive dogs running loose. At DAPS, we don't have the tools to deal with aggressive dogs. Animal Control is grateful to have us do as much as we can to lighten their load, which is substantial.

I asked around to find out who had been feeding the dog and was told Libby had been doing it. I didn't know Libby, but Jeannie did. She filled me in, and I realized I did know who she was though I had yet to actually meet her. Libby and her son Michael, who has a cognitive challenge, collected cans around Dixon. He was charming and said hello to everyone as he asked for recyclables. I called Libby to get more information on Danny and why the dog had been left in the house. It was she who told me the dog's name was Chata. Libby was amiable and concerned about Chata but didn't know what to do or who to call. She said Danny had gone to the hospital and had left her the food to feed every day, which she did until the food ran out. And that was at least two days ago. It was a good thing that Chata was chubby. It both kept her warm and from starving. Libby was pretty destitute and could not afford to buy extra food, so she just stopped going. She was also very angry with Danny for not returning when he said he would. I thanked Libby for caring for Chata as much as she could. I assured her that Chata was doing well and would go to a loving home soon.

At one time, Danny was an upstanding citizen; married with kids; had a decent job, and owned his home. Eventually, drugs got the better of him. His wife left. Danny was one of the locals barred from the Co-op, caught shoplifting one too many times. As he spiraled downward, the gas and electric were cut off at the house due to non-payment, and he took to sleeping at his friend Libby's house to get out of the cold, leaving the dog to fend for herself much of the time. Eventually, Libby had enough and told him to go.

It was time for me to deal with Danny. Being new to DAPS, I wanted to do this by the book. I wrote up a contract that released ownership of Chata to DAPS. Jeannie had said it really wasn't necessary. The dog was safe and would not be going back to Danny. Jeannie understood my desire to do this upfront and by the book and still tried to talk me out of it. I insisted, and Jeannie relented, asking if there was any way she could help. I really think she knew I needed the experience to learn how things work around here. I carried the paperwork around in my car because Danny was often out on the street and I figured I'd run into him at some point. I did, at the Post Office, about 6 weeks later. I recognized him from the time he came to the house looking for a handout using the name Michael. Danny appeared around the corner as I left the Post Office. He was wearing a plaid shirt and baggy jeans. I figured he had lost some weight from being in the hospital and from lack of money to buy food. I approached him, shaking with nerves but trying to remain calm. I wanted this to be a friendly and rational conversation about the dog. No question I was on edge, I now saw him as dangerous. I was grateful that we did finally meet in a public, open space. Had it not been, I would not have approached him. Enough people were coming and going that I felt if I were in trouble, there would be someone to help. I told Danny I had the dog. Not "his" dog, mind you. I asked him what the dog's name was. He said, "Chata." Chata means 'little friend.'" He told me how he loved Chata. "Um, no, you don't," I thought to myself. No one would do what he did to a dog they loved. Many people think love is a *feeling*. Love is a behavior. It is how we treat people or animals. I believe he loved having her around as she was now his only friend after Libby tossed him out. He really wanted her back, but there had been too much abuse and neglect for that to happen. Danny could not see that he neglected her. He had done his best but it fell short. My point of view is that people have choices; the animals don't. I, then, am the voice for the animals. I felt Chata had endured enough; it was time she had a stable home. I thought she'd agree. Chata. Sunshine. Good choice. I always try to choose a name with a similar sound when renaming a dog. I find the similarity helps the dog learn their new name more quickly. This time I got lucky!

I then told Danny that Chata was safe and being cared for and that I would like him to sign her over to DAPS since he was in violation of numerous county ordinances including neglect, abandonment, endangerment, not providing adequate food and shelter, the list went on. But he didn't see it that way. He wanted to know where she was. We don't disclose foster details to keep our volunteers safe. He then screamed at me, spitting in my face. "Give me my dog, or I'll sue you!" I thought that was pretty unlikely and legally as an officer in the rescue, I had indemnification so it wouldn't get far. I didn't see the need to have that discussion, so I said, "OK, we'll do it your way. We'll go to court, and I'll tell the judge about all of the violations that you've committed. That'll work." "I love my Chata," he said, a little calmer. "Anyone who loves their dog would not abandon her in a burned-out house that could collapse at any moment, in sub-zero temperatures," I pointed out. He didn't have a response other than assuring me that Libby had taken care of her. I told him what Libby had told me and he just looked at the ground. At that moment I think he recognized how much danger Chata had been in; that she could have died in the frigid temperatures; she was lucky to have survived.

People had stopped when they heard Danny yelling. They stood with me to show support and protection. That proved more than Danny could handle, and he walked away. Someone asked if I was OK. I was too shaken to register who it was that inquired. I said, "Yes, physically, anyway." "You know he's crazy." someone said. "Yes, I do," I replied quietly. I now knew it on a visceral level. I walked back to my car on wobbly knees. I knew the law was on my side, that he had no money for a lawsuit, and with the indemnification, I could not be sued personally. Still, he scared the bejeezus out of me. He could be violent with other men. Would he hit a woman? I didn't really want to find out. A psychotic on adrenalin has superpowers! I might not have had a chance. I took some comfort in never having raised my voice in response to anything he yelled or spat at me. I'm sure that made him even angrier, but like I said, I wanted it on my terms. And now wish I hadn't insisted on doing it by the book. A harsh lesson to learn. I hoped it would prove to be valuable one day.

I sat in my car for a few minutes before driving home, still feeling the adrenalin buzz of the confrontation. I wanted to fill my husband in on what had transpired. I really could use some support after that encounter. I needed a hug and time to process what had happened. As calmly as I could, I recounted the exchange with tears in my eyes. I asked for a hug. Instead of being supportive, he was angry! "You're going to get us sued!" he yelled. "No, he can't sue me, or us, I just told you that." was all I could say before he stormed off and into his office, slamming the door behind him. Wow. I was in shock, horrified by his response. Was it just that I was so upset after being verbally assaulted by Danny that this felt so harsh? I was starting to think not, but I really couldn't process anything more at that moment. I had gone completely numb.

Once I calmed down, I called animal control just to have a clear understanding of where we stood legally over taking possession of the dog. The Animal Control officer asked me a few questions; "Does the dog have a collar with an ID tag?" No. "Is she microchipped?" No. " Can he produce any vet records?" No. The simple answer, he told me, was, "Then she's not his dog." Legally Danny had no way to prove that he even owned a dog. If he wanted to go to court to try to take possession, he would be hit with the list of County Animal Ordinance violations and no judge would award him custody after what he did. I had a half-dozen witnesses to prove that she was abandoned in a burned-out house and photos and vet records to show the neglect. I don't think she was physically abused, beyond the toenails, as she didn't show any signs of trauma either physically or emotionally. For that, I was relieved. Chata was lucky to be alive and in the care of DAPS. Animal Control thanked me for handling the issue and offered us any help we might need. I didn't think we needed anything more. I called Jeannie to fill her in on what the officer had said and where we go from here. She reassured me that I personally could not be sued. DAPS could, but that was highly unlikely, and I shouldn't worry about it. DAPS had been threatened a few times over the years yet had never been sued. All were empty threats by desperate people who knew they didn't do right by their animals. All had insisted that they loved their pets.

In the unlikely event of a lawsuit, Jeannie would be there with me. I was pretty sure she and I would become good friends. I liked how she handled difficult situations in a very calm and matter of fact way. I think in rescue you have to be able to step back from the emotion or you just won't be in it for long. It will take its toll. I felt a little better and thought I had handled a difficult situation to the best of my ability. I couldn't ask any more of myself than that. I went to the kitchen and grabbed a beer. But the thought of my husband's complete lack of concern for my safety just wouldn't leave me.

I spent the next few months trying to find Sunshine the perfect home. She was sweet and such a laid back dog: house trained; didn't run off; came when called. She loved to get belly rubs and give kisses. Good with other dogs of all sizes; pretty much the perfect dog for just about anyone. Who wouldn't want this dog?! I had lined up three different, highly qualified, potential adopters, including one who owned a dog that looked exactly like her but was male. And his owner's name was Judy! How perfect! But the timing wasn't. I tried two others, but both of those fell through as well. One wanted a bigger dog; the other really wanted a younger purebred Chihuahua. Sunshine was middle-aged. A dog her size might live 20 years, but people have their wants, and I was really OK having her stay with me.

I did just recently try one more adoption. Ondrea contacted Jeannie via email looking for an older dog as a companion for her older dog. Jeannie forwarded the email to me to see if I knew of any dog that might fit. I immediately thought of Sunshine. She and Ondrea might be a perfect fit! I emailed Ondrea and discussed what she was looking for, and since it sounded like a perfect fit, we arranged a day to meet. I was so excited about Sunshine. This could be the adoption we were looking for!

Ondrea had some treats and other items she wanted to donate to the rescue. She and her husband Stephen had wanted to start their own rescue, but Stephen had recently died of cancer and running a rescue solo was too much. I met her at the Dixon Co-op. Sunshine rode in her lap as she followed me back to unload the donations. I had no idea that the truck was chock full of treats and beds and crates and all the things we so needed! After unloading, we sat and talked about the adoption. She really liked Sunshine and was going to come to pick her up after a short vacation. This sounded great. A few days later Ondrea emailed to tell me she couldn't take Sunshine. She had received a powerful psychic message that Sunshine's heart was with me and she just could not deny her that. I couldn't argue. This is how I have as many dogs as I do! Some connect so profoundly that they would not be happy anywhere else. I wonder if these are souls I have known before and they know they are home.

Sunshine is the only dog that sleeps on my bed. More than one usually causes fights or restless dogs that interrupt sleep, and I don't sleep well already, so disruptions are totally unwelcome. Each night Sunshine gives me a goodnight kiss, a sweet soft lick on the nose just like the night we pulled her out of the burned-out house. In the morning, she gently licks my face when she thinks it is time to get up. She is a joy. On the worst of days, she'll smile at me and gaze into my eyes, and things seem brighter. Most dogs will not keep eye contact. To them, eye contact is a threat or challenge. With Sunshine, it's like she is trying to speak to me, those enormous dark, dark orbs touching my soul, letting me know she is with me sharing her light. After that fourth failed attempt to adopt her out, I quit trying. Indeed, Sunshine was home.

What became of Danny? He died. In June 2014, I received the news. He had passed away a month or so earlier. I never did find out the details only that he was gone. Admittedly I felt relieved. The burned-out house still stands though it is starting to collapse. It now belongs to his daughter in Albuquerque, the one who we were told died of cancer. She is alive and well.

The Lone Dog Barks
by Hardik Vaidya

The lone dog barks,
In the pitch black of a night otherwise silent...

Photo by Judy Pearson

Boo

Pete had adopted Boo (short for Buddha) in the spring of 2012. Boo's story started with Gertie, her mom. Gertie was named after Gertrude Stein. Gertie was a pregnant stray that was most likely dumped at Jeannie's. Apparently, Gertie made her way down a long driveway to the trailer that sits between Jeannie's and my current home. There was a young woman who lived there, but she was a drug addict and not functioning well at the time. The young woman called Jeannie to say a mother dog had given birth under her trailer. She could hear the puppies squeaking, so she had been feeding them for a couple of weeks, but she wanted them gone. She was afraid of the mother. The mother dog was a beautiful olive-colored pit bull mix. Medium-sized and, like most mothers, very protective of her babies. Most mother dogs are. As soon as she could, Jeannie, with help from Therese (who named Gertie) went down to try to get her out from under the trailer. Therese was a self-proclaimed cat person. She had never had a dog but offered to foster Gertie until we could find a permanent home. And as is often the case, Therese fell madly in love with Gertie and adopted her. (You can read Therese's Gertie story on our website https://www.DAPSNM.org)

Once Gertie was out, it was time to retrieve the litter. They would be close to weaning age, perhaps old enough for adoption. When they pulled back the flap that allowed access under the trailer, they found that the puppies had died in the bitter cold. Unfortunately, Gertie had had her pups right before the brutal cold spell of 2012. The same one in which Sunshine was abandoned in the burned-out house. Five beautiful, frozen puppies were pulled out. What an awful sight. Especially for Therese as this was her first dog rescue. With heavy hearts, Jeannie headed home with the pups and Therese with Gertie.

Gertie began her new life with Therese. Having never had a dog, Therese had lots of questions! One of the biggest concerns was how the cats and Gertie would get along. I helped with an introduction and Gertie was not cat reactive - yeah Gertie! This would make the integration so much easier. The cats would still need some time to fully accept a dog in the house, but it went relatively smoothly. Then we received another call from the woman in the trailer. Apparently, there was one puppy that survived!! How was that possible? It had been brutally cold that week. Without the warmth of her mother, how on earth did this baby make it through this freeze? No time to spend pondering, this pup needed to be pulled ASAP! Jeannie and Bob went down with Bob's dog Trina, a large female German shepherd dog we had rescued six months earlier, and tried without success to get the puppy. Bob had tried to get Trina to go in under the home and retrieve the pup but to no avail. Neither Jeannie nor Bob were excited about crawling under the trailer to find the puppy. Jeannie called to see if I could give it a go. Maybe I'd have better luck. I said it was too late in the evening but first thing in the morning I'd go down and see what I could do.

As soon as it opened, I ran to the Co-op and grabbed a package of hot dogs, kosher beef hot dogs, and headed over. I stopped at Jeannie's to get Bob and the dog. Hannah, Bob and Jeannie's daughter, said she wanted to come too. I said, sure. We chatted as we headed down the long driveway to the trailer. What we talked about I have no recollection. If you have never been under one of

Boo 🐾

these trailers, I can assure you it was not a place I wanted to go. I'd crawled under a few to rescue puppies and, this one was particularly gross. It was too cold for spiders and snakes but rodents nested in the fiberglass insulation so mouse urine and droppings all around. They carry Hantavirus. A rare but potentially deadly virus, no thanks. There was also trash, old cans, building materials, and bags of who knows what kind of garbage tossed under the trailer and forgotten. Crawling through that was not on my list of things I needed to experience. I reached out and grabbed the flap that was the entry to the underbelly of the trailer. As I pulled it back, I turned to Trina and said, "Trina, go find the puppy." We could hear its whimpers, so we knew it was still alive. There was a bowl of partially eaten dog food just inside the flap. Jeannie and Bob had filled it the day before. It had clearly been visited; there was a divot where the pup had eaten. At least we assumed it was the puppy who ate it.

I looked at Bob; he was trying not to laugh. I could see he was thinking: "Trina won't do any such thing!" And in she went. His expression instantly changed to one of complete disbelief! Just then, the puppy was louder, much louder. I got down on my belly and stuck my head in right as Trina came out. She had gone in, located the pup, and either carried or pushed it toward the opening. The puppy was just inside the flap. She was loud, and she was strong! I coaxed her, and she came over willingly; a fat red and black pit mix. I grabbed her, tucking her inside my jacket. She was so cold! I turned and said: "Let's go. This baby needs to go to the vet ASAP." Bob still looked incredulous. I had to turn away to hide my grin.

As we headed back up to our road, Bob said, "I have a question." He paused. "How did you get Trina to do that for you? She's my dog, but she wouldn't go in for me yesterday!" he asked befuddled. I pulled the package out of my pocket, held it up, and said, "Ah! I have hot dogs! " I handed one to Trina, and she nearly took my hand with it. The bite hurt, but she didn't break the skin, and she hadn't bitten me on purpose. She just wanted her reward!

She'd earned it. I gave her another hot dog but made her sit and took care to not lose my fingers this time. As we reached the top of the drive, Bob and Hannah headed home, and I turned to get my car. I offered Bob the hot dogs, but he declined. Bob, Jeannie, and Hannah are all vegan or vegetarian. Hot dogs were not going home with them. I'm also vegetarian, but I use hot dogs to train dogs often; they work!

People who know me might tell you it wasn't the hot dogs at all that was the impetus for Trina going in under the trailer. And they may be right. We had rescued Trina from truly horrific abuse. Her previous owner went as far as hanging her from the top of a chain-link kennel to beat her. He thought it would make her aggressive. Thankfully he failed! Note: this was the worst abuse of an animal I have ever witnessed. It took some doing, but Jeannie convinced him to sell her the dog and release her to DAPS' care. Bob liked her immediately, and she became his dog. Trina was surprisingly well adjusted despite the beatings and has become a welcome addition to Jeannie and Bob's pack. She's an excellent guard dog as well. An imposing and loud presence, she is pretty scary if you don't know her. But back to the hot dogs. She may have done what I asked simply because I asked her to do it. She would have understood what I was feeling and thinking at the time and knew that the puppy needed to be rescued quickly. Plus, she's a shepherd. Her instincts to protect when the puppy started to whimper would have been undeniable. But as Bob had said she wouldn't go in for him and she did for me. This is just not unusual in my experience; you will see more examples in later rescues.

I held the pup in my lap on the way to the vet. I wanted her close to my warmth so she'd feel safe. I'd called ahead, and luckily, they could see her right away. She was a deep red color and very cute! Clearly, she was part pit bull, but I couldn't even start to guess what else. Her breed is what we call a Dixon Mix or a Northern New Mexico Trail Mix. They generally have some pit, heeler, shepherd, Rottweiler, Chihuahua, lab, hound, any breed really; and often a mix of many. I decided to call her Gwendolyn. It means blessed.

Though I am not a religious person, she was blessed with life for sure! Since her mother's name started with a G, I thought hers should too. It's a rescuer thing. Litters are often all named with names beginning with the same letter. Sometimes we choose a theme like flowers, cars, liquors, gemstones, etc. Gwen was happy to go for a ride. She switched back and forth from my lap to the blanket on the passenger seat. During the drive, she pottied on the blanket, and I could see it was mostly fiberglass insulation. Yuck! What was that doing to her insides?!

At the Vet clinic, she received a thorough exam and given an overall clean bill of health. She'd have to take some laxatives to clean out her belly and digestive tract, antibiotics to help heal her irritated insides and some probiotics to balance her gut microbes after the medications. In a few years, we might see the adverse effects of eating the insulation and whatever else she ate to stay alive. For now, she just needed to be home and adjust to life as a member of a family. My dogs thought she was great fun, particularly little Midnight, my seven-pound Yorkie-poo. They were almost the same size. Gwen wasn't quite old enough to start her shots, besides we wanted her to have some healing time before we began her first round. So she would have to stay inside for a few months. I set up a pen in my studio so she could be with the other dogs and me while I worked.

One day, Pete stopped by. The family - Pete, his sister Gina, and her husband Richard, and Gina and Pete's brother Chuc - bought the property next door together and had recently moved in. (The rest of the family would move here over the next few years.) Gina had a dog, a Golden Retriever, but Pete wanted a puppy of his own. Pete came by to ask me if I knew where he could find a puppy. He didn't yet understand my role in the rescue community; he would, soon enough. I took him to the living room where Gwen was sleeping in her other pen. "Yes, I do, right here!" came my response. The expression on his face was priceless. Somewhere between dumbfounded, and thinking I was magic.

I picked Gwen up and handed her to Pete. As he cradled her in his arms, I could just see what a great match this was. I filled him in on her story and informed him that we would not be reintroducing her to her mom at this time. Eventually, we would, but we wanted both to bond with their respective owners before we let them meet again. If he adopted her, I wanted him to be aware in case he ran into Therese and Gertie. Pete asked to take Gwen home and see how the resident dog, Trooper, did with her. He also wanted some time with her to see if he liked her temperament. I knew she wouldn't be coming back.

Pete called to ask if he had to bring her back. Smiling, I said: "No." He asked if he could change her name. I said, "of course! " He named her Boo, short for Buddha. I gave him the vet schedule for follow up and immunizations. Since he didn't have his car fixed yet, the next week, I took them both to the vet in Taos. It was a fun ride with Boo, and I had Pete listen to the sound my front wheel was making. He was good with cars and thought it sounded like a bearing. That was my thought as well, but it turned out I needed some brake work done.

Boo finished her shots at 16 weeks, and she was growing like a weed. Really like a puppy! As she got older, her coloring changed a bit, and she had a shepherd saddle in the fur on her back. Since she had been dumped and probably from a different community, we had no way of knowing what breed or mix, the dad was, but it was looking like at least some shepherd. When fully grown, her coat would lose the black saddle. She was a gorgeous deep, sienna red. She stayed a medium size and was built like a pit bull, strong! And she chewed like a pit bull. Pete called nearly every day with questions about training and how to deal with her chewing. Lots of chew toys in that house! For a little while, she was out of control. She clearly had some kind of herding breed in her as she would herd and grab everyone's ankles, sometimes hard! Pete worked with her daily. With his consistent training, she outgrew the negative behavior. I love it when an adopter wants to do the work! Often the dogs and puppies we rescue have lived through, or been subjected to, some pretty awful situations. That leaves them with some behavioral issues. Often with love, kindness, and consistency, they can overcome their past, but it takes work and patience. I was happy to help Pete and receive his daily calls. Boo socialized well with both people and other animals and grew into a sweet, friendly girl. Now in 2018, she is doing well. She had to be treated for liver damage from eating the insulation. Who knows what else she ate to fill her belly when she was under the trailer. It may ultimately shorten her life, but she will have lived a full life with a great family!

The Mother Cat
by Greg Richardson

The mother cat
grooms her kittens
who suck the sweet nectar
of her milk
and mew
in staccato.
Each one falls asleep
on her belly
as the contented mother
dreams
of birds and mice
and her own mother
long gone
serving as protector
of someone else's home.

Photo by Judy Pearson

Sabyl

I am not a cat lover. I like cats but, having grown up in a family in which we are all terribly allergic, we didn't have them. I couldn't spend a whole lot of time around them without suffering some moderately severe reactions. I would have nearly immediate asthma attacks that required a rescue inhaler. It was miserable. I have now lived with cats for 20 years, and I still am not a cat lover, though I no longer have severe reactions to the resident cats. It appears that after living with them for about two weeks, with full-on allergic reactions, my immune system cried uncle and gave it up. Quicker and cheaper than shots!

I find cats to be far more trouble than dogs. Anything on any surface is fair game. If it's not destroyed when the cats hurl it onto the floor, then one of dogs will surely find it and chew it into an unrecognizable mess before I even know it's missing! Work gloves (3 pairs!), prescription glasses, mail, animal prescription bottles, vases, coffee mugs, etc. all have been destroyed by the team of cats & dogs. None of it would have been damaged if I had just dogs.

Sabyl was a child of the corn, either abandoned or a runaway. I searched and posted and searched some more, but, I never found her owners. She was most likely out hunting to feed her kittens when I saw her. I would later learn what a skilled hunter she was. She appeared while I was out searching for a very different cat. Kim had called (yes that Kim, from the previous rescue.) Tom, Kim's cat, had not come home. He was a sweet black-and-white tuxedo, a good-sized, well-mannered boy. Tom always came when called. Kim's famous call "kitty kitty kitty kitty kitty kiiiiiiiitty!" (think Mini Pearl, you could hear it halfway across town) always brought him running, but not this time. Kim was distraught at the thought of losing him, so we went out in search of Tom. I had received another call, from Dana, that a black-and-white cat had been seen down on the Bosque. So that's where we headed. The Bosque is a beautiful flat wooded area down by the river, which runs nearly parallel to Hwy 75, it has two sides, east, and west, that are not connected. It was purposefully designed that way to limit vehicle access. It is lush and green and many farm the fertile soil there. We headed to the west side where the cat sightings had occurred. Kim lives on the west side but right on highway 75. She shares a home with her mother Hallie, numerous dogs, a few cats and dozens of birds.

Kim and I both set out calling for Tom, but there was no sign of him. We moved down the road a bit and kept calling, hoping he'd come out from wherever he was hiding. I was in a yard next to a large garden with tall, dry corn stalks; suddenly, I heard what I thought to be a faint meow. I didn't see a cat, but I listened to another very soft meow. It was tough to hear over the rustling cornstalks shaking in the wind. Standing utterly still; just listening...there was a soft rustle; clearly, there was a cat in the corn! Very cautiously, a little black and white cat appeared. The small cat was shy but very sweet. I called to Kim that I found him! As I pulled this little cat out of the corn and held it up, it became immediately evident that it wasn't a "him." It was a "her." A pregnant her; still just a kitten herself. With feral cats, this is often the way it goes - pregnant on their first heat and perpetually pregnant forever after. I put her in the crate I had brought and went to find Kim. She was so disappointed that it wasn't Tom. We had had such hopes. A storm was blowing in, and I needed to get this momma to the vet, so we called it a day. It was clearly far too late to have her spayed so she would come and live with me and have her kittens in my office. My office is small and warm; an excellent whelping room. Or queening room in this case. Dogs whelp, cats queen - both mean "to give birth."

I called the vet and Doc said to bring her right in. She examined the little momma cat and said, "No, she's not pregnant, but she has recently had kittens. Keep her overnight and in the morning take her back to where you found her; she will lead you to her kittens." On the way home, I named her Sabyl because she looked like a sable. She had a black smoke coat with white toes on a couple of her feet. An absolutely beautiful cat with medium long hair, shiny black, but her undercoat was a warm smoky grey. I don't think I'd ever seen a cat like her. I made her a comfortable bed in my office with a littler pan and a low-sided box to keep the kittens in. The next morning when the sun came up, I put her in the crate and took her back where we found her. Sure enough, she trotted right over to the place she had the kittens hidden. I had to follow her across a large yard, through a thicket, easy for Sabyl, and halfway up a driveway into another property. As soon as they heard their momma's meow out popped three beautiful little kittens. They had been hiding in a woodpile on the back of a house. It was built to stop erosion as the land, and the neighbor's farm, were at very different elevations. Sabyl and family were on the neighbor's property. Luckily the neighbor was in Santa Fe for an extended period.

The kittens' eyes were open, so they were about two weeks old. The two boys were a soft smokey grey with white markings, and the third was a little girl that looked very much like her mom. They were born in the wild, so even at this very young age, they were feral. Having had no human contact, they were very wary and would not allow me to pet or handle them. I wanted to try to gain their trust before resorting to trapping as that can traumatize them.

I wanted them to trust me so that they could be socialized. We'd have them spayed or neutered and adopted out into good homes.

For the next couple of weeks, I was over on the property twice a day for feeding and just to be in their space so they would eventually socialize to humans. They were so very wary. It would take time and patience. The driveway was 50 yards long through the tall cottonwoods that so love the moisture of the Bosque. The sunlight filtered through the trees, and the wind made such a beautiful whisper with the leaves. I always felt it was welcoming me back; so beautiful and peaceful. I really enjoyed going down to feed the family every day. It was such a pleasant respite from the busyness of my days. The feeling of calm seeped in as soon as I arrived. The sounds and smells so different from my house, which sat above the acequia, where it was arid. Our property had water rights, but the water had to be pumped to irrigate. Anything below the ditch, like the next-door neighbor's property, was very fertile and lush. My property was also wide open to the brutal summer sun. With few trees other than what was planted near, or grew on the banks of, the acequia. Here on the Bosque everything was lush, shaded and closed in by green growth.

One evening I was later than usual, and it was fast approaching dark. I asked my husband to go with me since I wasn't comfortable being down there alone after dark. We have bear, mountain lions, bobcats; I didn't want to run into any of them alone. He said he'd go with me this time. On the way over, I talked about what I was doing. My husband asked how long it would take to catch the kittens. I said I'd hoped not more than about two weeks. He didn't seem happy with that answer, saying something about the time it would take feeding them twice a day for another two weeks. I understood it was a lot of work, but these things happen on their own time line, not mine. "It can't be rushed, or I lose the trust I've gained," I replied. He just made some noise that indicated he wasn't pleased or thought I was ridiculous or both. I thought it would be good for him to meet Sabyl. My husband is a cat lover, and he could see what it is I do on these rescues. I have a fiercely independent streak, born out of necessity, that can be difficult for some men. It was one of the issues to which I was trying to pay more attention. I intended to make him feel needed and included, but he wasn't terribly interested. He didn't seem to see the beauty that surrounded us. The light, the sounds, a mother cat and kittens who would be saved. Or that I was grateful to have him along at that late hour. I was trying to connect but feeling thwarted.

Sabyl was amazing! She came when I called, just like a dog. And so affectionate. My husband took an immediate liking to her. She was tiny and beautiful and so very sweet. She ran up to me and rubbed my leg, and together we walked back to the woodpile to eat. I thought it was a beautiful moment. That was the only time my husband came with me. The scene repeated each day, twice a day, rain or shine, with Sabyl running to greet me from somewhere in the lush growth and escorting me to the kittens. Who wouldn't love this cat? I did, and I wasn't a cat person! It wasn't long before Sabyl allowed me to approach the kittens; I had her trust. She would rub against me and let me stroke her when I sat to feed her babies. But the kittens weren't so easy. They would pop out, see me, and pop right back in! I gave them a wide berth so they would come out and eat, but it was clear they were not going to allow me to get too close any time soon. After a couple of weeks, it was becoming a concern that if the kittens remained here then they would indeed be feral and I really wanted to socialize them. It was at about this time that Sabyl relocated the kittens. Mother cats will do this even in a domestic situation. After a few weeks, they will move the kittens to keep them safe. Sabyl was a good mom. Thankfully it didn't take too long to find them as they were now old enough to go out to explore.

Sabyl had moved them from the woodpile up into the thicket behind the house. A smart girl, as this gave them excellent protection. It was, of course, harder for me to get to them. I had to crawl through the prickly briars to an open space where the kittens played. But, they were closer to people! After a few days of feeding them there, I was finally able to handle one of the boys! He was far less skittish than the other two, so he came home with me one afternoon. The next day I set a trap for the other two. It didn't take long to catch the kittens; just two days to get the remaining two. I had some concerns about their attitude toward me since I had to use the trap. I brought them home, and to my surprise, they seemed content to be there.

Now we had to get mom. Without the kittens around, she was far less interested in my company! We left a carrier with cat food in it at Dana's house. Sabyl would eat her meals in her crate right by Dana's front door. Within a couple of days, Dana just closed the door on the carrier when Sabyl was eating and called me to come get her. I brought her home, and she settled in with the kittens. She made herself at home as if she'd always been there. That convinced me that she was once someone's pet. We put up notices to see if we could find her previous owner; no one responded. They all stayed with me in my office away from the dogs. And they were welcome to stay as long as necessary.

Having them home, I could continue to socialize them, learn their behavior, and name them. I called the boys Cindar (Spanish for cinder) and Ash since they were smoky grey. And the little girl Tiznara. Tiznara means "to darken." She was a smoke, like her mom, but quite a bit darker. At first, they hid and were reluctant to let me handle them, except Ash, he was the friendly one. With a little time they socialized; they became very playful and sought my attention. They were then about 4 weeks old and growing like crazy. Cindar was huge! Ash was fairly average in size, and Tiznara was petite like her mom. They would nurse for another couple of weeks and then Sabyl and I would start to wean them.

During this time, I received a call from one of our vets about the possibility of Sabyl being a surrogate, not once, but twice! Both times for abandoned kittens. They asked if I thought Sabyl would take another kitten to nurse. I said there is only one way to find out!

The first kitten was a little grey, tabby boy. We named him Squeaky. He didn't meow so much as squeaked. He was just about the same age as Sabyl's kittens. Squeaky was found running on the road all alone. No sign of any other kittens or a momma cat. He may have been dumped with the expectation that he would quickly be run over.

The second call came just a few days later. This time a little female. She was a very sick little kitty. She wasn't doing well at all and weighed only a few ounces. She was the runt of a feral litter out of Chamita, a community outside Española. We named her Chamita, which means "little friend." She and her brother, who did not survive, had been abandoned by their mother. Without her mother and brother we didn't think the tiny kitten would live much longer even with a surrogate. Much to our surprise, with the mothering from Sabyl and the warmth of her new siblings, she thrived!

Once again, Sabyl was my hero. She cleaned Chamita and kept her close. Sabyl knew precisely what to do. She seemed to know that this little one needed extra care. She treated Chamita like she was her own. Chamita was quite a bit younger than Sabyl's kittens and much smaller, but she joined right in. Sabyl was a fantastic adoptive mom. You might think that any cat would do this, but that is not the case. Often a potential surrogate will kill another mother's kittens because they are perceived as a threat to their own litter. I do think Sabyl understood how weak Chamita was and how much she was needed. I may not like cats, but I loved this one!

The kittens all hung out in my office until they were old enough to go to new homes. We generally keep them until at least 8 weeks, 10-12 if possible, so they are well socialized and cared for by the mother cat or dog. Chamita went back to Maria's in Chamita as a house cat. No more wild life for her! Cindar and Ash went together to a local mechanic's garage. The garage is on the same property as the house, and Gary and his wife, Debbie, are long-time rescuers.

The boys would have a place to live and hunt and be cared for. Tiznara went to a family with small children. She was tiny and sweet, so it was a good fit for little ones. Sabyl? Well, by now I was totally taken with this beautiful girl, so she stayed with me as an indoor/outdoor cat. She was an incredibly good hunter but liked her lap time too. We had lost our other cats shortly after moving in. All three were indoor cats. Within a few weeks they all ran away. Sabyl would help fill the void of that loss. She would be my new cat, at least for now.

Kim continued her search for Tom but he was never found.

Healing Hands
by Aldo Kraas

I have the healing hands
Let me put my healing hands
Where you are feeling the pain
And you will see that it will go away
Like a miracle made in heaven

Photo By Judy Pearson

Turnip

Turnip (or Turnup, more on that later) had a thing for cars. Not the typical chase anything that moves kind of thing dogs have for cars. She doesn't chase them; she chose to live under one! It was late winter 2013 when Ki and Kai, a wonderful couple who owns a favorite local restaurant up in Peñasco called *Sugar Nymphs*, called for help. Kai called to tell me that they had discovered a puppy living under an abandoned car at the end of their driveway.

The car was parked out close to the road; the house sat at the far end of the driveway. Kai said the puppy had been there for about a month. I could see how Ki and Kai might not notice that they had a squatter, so the puppy may have been there for some time. They didn't know if it was a boy or a girl, but it was a brindle; breed mix unknown. They thought the puppy was just a couple of months old. Try as they might they couldn't get it to come out from under the car and were getting concerned. They had been feeding it, giving treats, even singing to it and still, the puppy would not budge. It would briefly peek out and show its face, but that was it. Kai asked what we, DAPS, could possibly do. I told her that I would come up with some extra special treats like cheese and hot dogs and see if I could get under the car and get the puppy out.

There was still ice and snow on the ground, but it was warming up, so it was ice and snow and mud. Lots of mud. I wore hiking clothes that I didn't mind if they got covered in mud, and might make it easier to slide under the car. The house is off the beaten path down a winding dirt road. As I drove up, I wondered what the puppy might be. Pit bulls can be brindle as can boxers and other mastiff breeds. Chances were it was what we refer to as a northern New Mexico mix or a Dixon Trail mix, a multi-breed mix better known as a mutt. It wasn't that the breed mattered, I am a fan of pit bulls, and I love boxers, so whatever it was - fine by me.

We just needed to get this baby out, to the Vet and into a good home. I pulled into the driveway, and there was the car. I did not go to the house first as I thought Kai would just come out when she wanted. I had called to let her know I was headed out. I parked myself by the car, I'm unsure what make it was, a Fiat perhaps, something small and low to the ground. It sat only about 8 or 10 inches off the ground. I got down low on my belly and peered under. I could see the pup but could not tell the breed or the gender. It was clearly scared. Not wanting to frighten it more, I laid out some treats to entice it out. It would only come out about halfway, grab the goods, then scoot right back under. After about an hour of this game, I only succeeded in getting the puppy all the way out once. But I had her long enough to see that it was a girl. This beautiful baby girl was petrified! I decided to try to crawl under the car. I got back down on my belly and slithered in the mud under the vehicle. It was a tight fit! Thankfully, the ground was soft and slippery. It was also cold and wet, icy and muddy!

As small as I am, I could only get about half way in. Smart pup! Not much was going to fit under there and give her trouble! I was in far enough to see where the puppy had been living. She had created a cozy little den at the front end where the tarp covering the car made a space much like a tent. The sun was shining, and the orange tarp was translucent, so the interior had a beautiful warm glow. A solar dog house! It is probably what saved this little girl during the cold of winter. The puppy had collected all sorts of junk and brought it home. Everything from yogurt containers to boxes, plastic bags, a shoe, a glove, all kinds of trash, sticks, cardboard, you name it. She seemed quite proud of her collection. As I lie in the mud under the car, she brought me pieces of junk! Ki and Kai had given her some bedding, so she really was living in the lap of junk luxury. I imagined that she would sneak out at night to collect whatever she could find to eat, and if it wasn't edible, she brought it back anyway.

I coaxed the puppy over with some treats. Finally, I was able to touch the tiny pup. I stroked her and gave her a pile of hot dogs while talking soft baby talk to help calm her. She devoured the treats. She allowed me to hold her so, it was time. When I tried to pull her out from under the car, she let out a bloodcurdling scream! It startled me; I wasn't prepared for that! But I did not let go. I held her close to give her comfort and whispered that it was OK and that it gets better from here. She was the most beautiful puppy I've ever seen. She was a tiger striped brindle boxer mix. Mixed with what, I didn't know. But her coat was silky and soft like no puppy coat I'd ever touched. Her sweet frightened face just made my heart ache. We will never know the extent of the trauma and abuse that this puppy suffered, but it quickly became evident that she had been severely abused. There were no new injuries, but evidence of old injuries was there, and her abject fear of people was so deep. I tried to wrap my head around what kind of cold-hearted beast would abuse such a beautiful, innocent little pup. I decided I didn't really want to know.

While still under the car I heard a voice. "How long have you been here?" Kai asked. "Oh, about an hour," I replied. She said she thought I'd gotten lost but decided to come to look to see if I was here. Kai had brought a crate out with her. I wasn't sure that introducing Turnip to it was going to go well, but she ran right in! Clearly feeling safe in an enclosed space. Dogs are den animals, and Turnip had quite the den, but she just seemed to love this crate from the get-go.

Ki and Kai had named her Turnup because she just "turned up!" I preferred the spelling like the vegetable, Turnip because Turnup looks too much like tuneup. Although she did live under the front end of a car! But I thought since Ki and Kai were chefs, the vegetable fit also. From there, the plan was to introduce Turnip to the resident alpha female Delilah and see if she would accept a puppy. They really wanted to keep this puppy, but Delilah wasn't good with other dogs. I had had an alpha female years ago that was also not good with other dogs, though she loved puppies! So, we had our fingers crossed that it might work. We allowed Delilah to just sniff Turnip in the crate. That way if there were any signs of aggression, Turnip would be safe and protected. I watched closely to see what Delilah would do. She walked over, looking curiously at the crate, and sniffed. I didn't like her body language. I watched her little stub tail twitch. It didn't wiggle, it didn't wag, it twitched. That's a sign of aggression, I knew Ki and Kai would not take any chances and, if there was any overt sign of aggression, it was a no go. We then proceeded with great caution. The next step was an on-leash introduction. I wasn't optimistic, but we needed to see for sure, and I would keep Turnip safe. I put her on a leash and from a safe distance, let them size the other up. Delilah curled back her lips and started to growl. At that point, it was abundantly clear we were not going to go any further. There was no way Delilah was going to be OK with this puppy on her turf. I was relieved that we were all seeing the aggression, and there was no question about how Delilah felt. Turnip retreated to the safety of her crate, smart girl! So then Ki asked, "Now what do we do?" I said, "Well, let me take her home to be with my gang and see if she can socialize into the pack and socialize to humans." My great hope was that with time, she would learn to trust humans again. It would take some effort but in a stable home with a generally quiet man, my husband, and lots of canine friends to show her the ropes she might just blossom.

Turnip was happy to be back in her crate, and we loaded up and headed home. I felt terrible that it didn't work out with Delilah. Ki & Kai had fallen in love with this girl. I could see why.

On the way home, I continued to pet the puppy through the openings in her crate. I talked to her to reassure her that everything was OK and going to get better. She licked my fingers and rubbed against them. This was a good sign. It seemed to me she was conveying an understanding that she was safe. We arrived home, and I introduced her to my indoor dogs one by one. Meeting them all at once would be too overwhelming even with the most socialized puppy. She did OK! Better than expected actually.

There were no signs of aggression from any of my dogs, and Turnip showed none either. Lots of butt sniffing and licking and sizing each other up. It was fun to watch. My indoor dogs were generally pretty friendly and happy to meet new friends. We all headed out to the yard where they could run and play freely. Turnip was still frightened, but it looked like she was going to settle in and learn to be a family dog. As the dogs were running around, I noticed that Turnip could not keep up. She walked with an odd gate and had a difficult time running. I watched her move and tried to figure out what was wrong. She seemed to not stand or walk on fully extended legs. She kind of squatted. Of course! She had spent so much time under the car where she could not fully stand that the muscles in her legs were unable to straighten. I wasn't terribly concerned but would check it out with the Vet. I suspected now that she had the freedom to run her legs would gain strength quickly.

At first, she kept to herself, but a couple of the dogs would not take no for an answer when they wanted to play. Sunshine seemed to take a liking to Turnip. Since Sunshine was so easy going Turnip allowed her closeness. They would become good friends. After a few weeks, she was playing with the other dogs, hanging out on the sofa, and she was learning to trust people. She was a voracious eater, many abandoned dogs are. They live without enough food for too long then in a home environment, it takes time to learn that the food always gets refilled. For Turnip, it also left her with some food aggression. To keep the peace, she was fed away from the other dogs. At treat time, I had all of the dogs sit for their treats. One by one, they received their reward. It took Turnip no time to follow the pack, and treat time was without incident.

I still didn't know how she was going to do with people. She was doing fine with me, as is often the case with shy dogs. There is something about me that allows them to relax and feel safe. She met my husband and did keep her distance. I knew that it might take some time for her to be comfortable with any man. But we'd work on that. I already had too many dogs, and it wasn't my intention to keep Turnip beyond fostering and socializing. My husband and I had that conversation. He often didn't have a choice when a rescue needed a place to go, they came to our house. This wasn't always easy for him.

In some cases, I could find someone to foster a dog until we could adopt them out or get them on transfer, but in this case, I knew she needed to be with me. She already felt safe and to deny her that after what she lived through? I couldn't do it. So it was vital that she be exposed to kind people and learn that they are not going to hurt her. Those days were behind her. I had her vetted; shots, exam, and scheduled for a spay. During the appointment, we discovered that this tiny three-month-old puppy was actually six months old! To determine a dog's age, we do an examination of their teeth. Puppies start to lose teeth at four months of age and have a full set of adult teeth by about six months. Turnip had all of her adult teeth.

I couldn't believe it. A six-month-old boxer mix should be twice her size. Well, unless she was half Chihuahua! I didn't think that was the mix, she didn't look like a Chihuahua, but anything could be in her DNA. Perhaps as she grew, it would become apparent what the other breed(s) were. For now, I could only say she was

Turnip 🐾

obviously predominantly boxer. I had the Vet look at her funny gait and leg strength, but it hadn't taken long for her to start to walk normally, so the Vet had no concerns. Turnip was surprisingly healthy, considering the circumstances she had been living under. The only adverse effect was that her growth had been stunted due to malnutrition, which was what I suspected. We wondered how big she would get if she is this small at six months.

Turnip was smart and easily trained, but the food aggression issue at mealtime would not be solved quickly. She ate well and grew fast but would always be smaller than if she had had proper early nutrition. Her coat was shiny, and she was adjusting to home life. She was still shy and nervous, especially around new people, men more than women, but I was working hard to help her past her trauma. When I first brought her home, I had a conversation with my husband about the kinds of abuse and injury she may have suffered, most likely at the hands of a man. We had an opportunity to help her heal so she could be adopted out to a loving family. Depending on how she did, she may only be able to be with a woman or women; it would take time to know. She would need to be treated with patience and loving kindness. No raised voices, no raised hands or sudden movements, only gentleness so she could learn to trust people again, particularly men. We had an opportunity here to make a difference for this beautiful pup.

A few months later, as I pulled in the driveway, Turnip came home after being out and about, frothing at the mouth and shaking. I looked at her eyes, and they were in Nystagmus. Nystagmus is a rapid uncontrolled eye movement. I grabbed the phone and called the Vet for an emergency appointment. After giving a brief description of what was happening, they said they would be on standby for our arrival. Her symptoms indicated some type of poisoning. But what? Her blood work indicated an acute poisoning. Her liver count was literally off the charts. What kind of poisoning would cause these symptoms? It was not like rodent poison. The veterinarian suspected it was mushrooms. Perhaps from the trash. We had no way of knowing. She was put on IV fluids and had her stomach flushed. By the next day, her liver counts were better; it looked like she'd make a full recovery though she could have liver problems down the road. I searched the yard and did find some trash that was most likely pulled from the neighbor's trash can but couldn't identify the contents. I'd never get an answer. She made a full recovery and has so far not shown any signs of lasting health issues. She weighs about 55 pounds now. Turnip spends much of her time in the yard playing with her toys during the day; then comes in at night to hang out on the sofa.

That Christmas I was wrapping presents, and I ran out of paper. I picked up the cardboard tube to toss to the dogs in the living room, they loved cardboard tubes as a chew toy. Turnip was right by my side, she panicked, tucked tail, and flew out of the dining room in terror. That made it pretty clear that she been hit with a broom or a stick, something cylindrical. Even though I knew she had been hit, it caught me by surprise how visceral her reaction was. My heart ached for her. I could feel what she must have felt when being abused and went to reassure her with soft words and a loving touch. She licked my face as I apologized for scaring her. Would she ever fully heal? I didn't think so, but I was determined to give her the opportunity.

I stroked and hugged her as I handed the tube to the other dogs so that she could see that it wasn't something to be afraid of, it was a toy. One she could take and shred. If she could destroy it, I hoped it would give her some sense of power over the abuse objects she once endured. It would take some time for her to overcome these fears, but she's never overcome all of them. That's one reason why she stayed with me. I don't know how she would do with someone else who doesn't understand trauma. I knew she trusted me, and I didn't want to break that trust.

When it became evident that Turnip was going to be staying, my husband requested that I not adopt anymore dogs. I wanted him to know I respected that he had hit a limit. We had eight or nine dogs at the time, and that was more than enough. I agreed, no more dogs. But as you can imagine that was about to change.

One morning in May, while I was making pancakes for breakfast, I saw Turnip jump up on my husband. She had her front paws up on his hip to say hello. I smiled thinking great, she wants to interact! Instead of taking the opportunity to teach her to sit, not jump, and treat her with loving kindness, he became angry and used bodily force to move her off. She immediately sat down, trembling, eyes wide. I'm sure she was anticipating being hit. I looked at my husband and said very calmly, "Don't kick the dog." He turned to me enraged, with clenched and shaking fists, and demanded that I treat him with kindness. (We had just been given the assignment to read The Power of Kindness by Piero Ferrucci in our counseling. It is a beautiful little book. It makes the point that being kind to others is, in essence, showing ourselves kindness. I've said before if you haven't read it is worth your time.) I told him that I hadn't been unkind to him. But, he certainly had been unkind to the puppy. The yelling continued; I told him he needed to come and sit down. We needed to talk. I was, and still am, amazed at how calm and collected I was. I had been working toward building the marriage, but of late, my focus had been changing. The question had become was I willing to stay in the marriage? It was evident that my husband didn't have the courage to end it, nor the ability to have a frank discussion about leaving me for another woman. I was left with no choice. That day I ended our marriage.

Those of us who are in rescue are here because we cannot *not* be. There is a deep soul connection that cannot be denied. Trust me, I've tried. There is a level of compassion that many do not possess, nor do they understand it. For some people compassion is a learned response, for some it cannot be learned. For us it is deeply ingrained, part of who we are. We cannot unlearn it. An animal in need calls us to act. Once we rescue them it is our responsibility to care for and protect them. To us a house full of critters is a beautiful, loving, soul filling thing. For others it is simply a pain in the rear end. It is chaotic and messy, loud and a huge responsibility. To a rescuer it is heaven. To a non-rescuer it can be frustrating to the point of anger. The partner of a rescuer can feel jealous, overwhelmed and a loss of control. To go into that further would be another book. Suffice it to say that the two are essentially incompatible. The rescuer cannot fathom the lack of compassion and sees rescuing as their soul work, their duty, and the beauty of it all. The non-rescuer cannot grasp any of that. And that only fuels the frustration and they end up despising the animals and the rescuer for who and what they are.

It took me until now, writing the book, to fully understand the gravity of the situation. At the time I just knew we were approaching a flash point and nothing was going to change it; it would never get better.

The separation papers were filed days later, and I requested that all weapons be removed from the home. Mutual friends agreed to hold them. All guns were transferred except one. When my father-in-law passed away, each family member was allowed to choose from his gun collection. Mine was a pistol. Actually a small revolver. I am not pro-gun, though I have a healthy respect for them. I grew up in a home with several kinds of firearms. My father was a marksman in the Army, and we would target shoot. I had never thought about shooting anything living, but I felt out here I might use one against a coyote or bear if they threatened the animals. My gun could not be found. It had been put away in the attic, but neither of us was able to locate it. I had searched the attic, twice, to no avail. I hoped that was true for us both. I was instructed by my attorney, and our therapist, to file an animal abuse report with the Police in case the behavior escalated. Both had concerns that I might be in danger. The mistreatment of animals is often the precursor to domestic violence. If there is a report on file, they take domestic violence much more seriously. We have a center in Taos, Community Against Violence or CAV, and I made an appointment with them as well. They talked to me about an exit strategy and instructed me to keep a diary of behaviors and/or threats. As well as set up a network of friends who could jump in and help if needed. I never thought I would be in this position. I was scared but prepared. No one knew what would happen if he lost control.

When we divorced, Albert stayed with my ex-husband. The rest of the dogs went with me. Albert was the only dog my ex wanted, and the only one he had adopted. Sabyl also stayed even though she was my cat and a DAPS cat. She and Albert adored each other. She would bring him dead animals and birds as a token of her love. They were best friends. I just didn't have the heart to break them up. I was also concerned that I'd lose her if she moved with me, figuring she'd try to find her way back to Albert. It was a massive risk, so Sabyl stayed with her beloved Albert. I miss them both. Sabyl was not like any other cat I'd had or known. She was wild and free but came when called, like a dog, and loved attention. She was fiercely loyal, to both her dog and human. It was painful to leave her behind, but losing her would be worse. Besides, she had her Albert to take care of, and he, her.

Turnip ended up staying with me, she just didn't do well with other people. I didn't think I could find anyone with whom she would feel safe. She was now attached to me, and I doubted she would bond with someone else. Perhaps in time she would heal, and I could find her a good match, but for now, it was too traumatic to consider, for either one of us. In the divorce settlement, I received a little money but had no idea where I would find something I could afford or in the short time I was given. During packing to move, a double wide on the far side of town went on the market. It was far more than I could afford, but the owner had an idea, he would split the property into two lots. Brilliant! I had to pay outright, but it was a great place to be. It was right next door to the Executive Director of the Rescue! We could easily share animal care. And it was beautiful, quiet, and had great neighbors.

When I moved to the new house, Turnip became very protective. Jeannie, my next-door neighbor, and my Executive Director had some concerns that we might have to put her down. None of us quite understood why Turnip's personality changed with the move other than she felt she needed to protect me. I liked having a watchdog, but I didn't need protecting from Jeannie! One day while caring for the animals at my place, Jeannie discovered that if she approached Turnip through the back door of the house rather than the gate of the fenced yard, Turnip was friendly! Turnip understood that Jeannie wasn't a threat when she came through the house. From then on all was well; Turnip returned to being her sweet but shy self around Jeannie. About a year after I moved, I had an absolutely gorgeous puppy dumped near my house. This happens fairly often. People who don't want their puppies know that if they drop them here, we will take them in and find them homes. This new puppy appeared to be a shepherd/lab mix, and Turnip took to her instantly. I named the puppy Aurora. She and Turnip were the absolute best of friends and had the run of the fenced-in yard. Aurora was significantly larger than Turnip, but Turnip was still the boss. Until the fights began.

One day I heard the unmistakable sound of a serious dog fight in the back yard. I ran out and grabbed them each by the collar and held them apart. Note: don't ever do this!!! It is an excellent way to get badly bitten. Thankfully they did not bite me. They settled down, and life was quiet, for a while. After the fourth fight, I called Jeannie to tell her we needed to make a change. I was afraid they would escalate into a deadly altercation. No one wanted that. We moved Aurora next door to be with Trina at Jeannie and Bob's. There has never been a fight between them.

"i Feel Your Brilliance"
by Lisa Visor

I feel your brilliance
as you lean into me
seductively playing
upon my bare skin
an endless dance beyond space
beyond time . . .

Photo by Judy Pearson

Albert

Albert had an appointment at the Dentist's office one Tuesday morning in mid-March of 2013. It was just a few weeks after Turnip had arrived and I had promised my husband I wouldn't adopt any more dogs. I was doing my best to consider his viewpoint. We were in counseling to try to strengthen the marriage, so no more dogs; agreed.

I was resting at home, trying to kill a cold. At the end of the week, we were headed to Italy for our nephew's wedding. A week in Tuscany! The last thing I wanted was to travel with a cold, so I was laying low, taking immune-boosting herbs, lots of fluids and rest. The phone rang; it was my friend Violet. She asked, "Are you busy?" I said, "No, I'm just resting trying to kill a cold before we leave for Italy. Why? What's up?" "Could you help me with a dog?" she inquired. I asked her to tell me more.

There was a dog out on the highway for the last couple of weeks, and he apparently had a schedule. At 11:30, he was at the Dental Clinic; at noon, at the road construction site where the guys shared their lunch with him. By 12:30 he was checking the mail at the Embudo Post Office and around one o'clock, was down at Toby's house on County Road 62. Toby's was down off the main highway in a wooded neighborhood. Toby was a large brindle mixed breed; we had a few like him around town, and he was Albert's best buddy. Albert made this circuit every day like clockwork. Violet had been watching him. It was around 11 am when she called, so Albert was due at the Dentist. I headed out with numerous treats in hand; cheese, meat, doggy junk food; you name it, I had it! I also had a collar and a leash in the car. Violet had said she thought he was a St. Bernard mix, so a big dog. I pulled in just about the time Albert arrived at the Dentist. He was easy to identify! He was a big, fluffy, black-and-white boy, and when I got close enough, it was quite clear that he was a Landseer (Newfoundland) cross. The crossbreed may have been border collie, but around here anything is possible. He was shy, but he didn't show any signs of aggression. I tried to approach him; he liked to keep his distance. I wasn't going to push it. I didn't want to scare him off, so Violet and I sat there, on the side of the driveway to the Dentist's Office, feeding him treats and chatting. I filled her in on my upcoming trip; who would be taking care of the animals, and general life in Dixon stuff. I alternated between talking to the dog, generally trying to convince him that he needed a collar, and talking with Violet. All the while tossing him tasty morsels. I wanted to know the dog's story, but he wasn't as interested in talking to me as he was into getting the treats. Each time that he took a reward was an opportunity to make contact. A non-threatening approach is to pet a dog under the chin. Coming over the head of many dogs, particularly shy or fearful ones, will get you nowhere, or bitten. The best way to approach any dog is to squat down, so you are not above them at all. It's one reason we were sitting while treating and chatting. We didn't relax until I was comfortable that he wasn't aggressive since sitting put us in a vulnerable position. This guy wasn't really shy or fearful, just wary. Who knows what he had been through! In a relatively short while he allowed me to pet him, not get too close, pretty much at arm's length, but pet him. We were making some progress! After about an hour of treating and petting, I wasn't able to get any closer to him, so no collar, yet. He did sniff the collar I held out for him, but any attempt to put it around his head resulted in him backing away. With no collar, I couldn't get him in a car, and I was out of treats, so I headed home to restock. By the time I got back, he had moved on. He wasn't at the Post Office; after a short search, we found him at Toby's. Toby lived down the road across from the Post Office which was on the main highway in the area, State Highway 68. Like 75, the main thoroughfare through Dixon, 68 was two lanes, but the speed limit was 55, so a reasonably dangerous place for the dog to be hanging around and crossing throughout the day. Most of the side roads were poorly paved or dirt, or some combination of both. County Road 62 was both.

We went that way because it was near the Post Office and as Violet had watched the dog's activity, she thought that might be where he headed. We asked the construction workers if they had seen where the dog went and sure enough they pointed across the highway. Chuckling at the dog's regularity, we headed down 62. This was a heavily wooded road. Since it was close to the river, the cottonwoods grew thick and tall. There were plenty of places for a dog to hide, but as we rounded the bend, there they were lying in the yard in the shade just hanging out. Toby was not as large but was just as gentle as the big guy. With our arrival, Toby's owner came out and introduced himself. He told us the dog had been visiting for a couple of weeks. He introduced me to Toby and said he was happy to have a friend. I asked if he would like to keep the dog, and DAPS would get him neutered and up to date on shots. He said no. I didn't really expect any other answer, but I was still disappointed.

This close to an international trip and fighting a cold I just didn't need the hassle of a foster dog - especially not one this big. I told Toby's owner that we were trying to get a collar on the new dog to get him to the vet and into a new home if we couldn't find his owner. The usual protocol with a stray as required by County Ordinance is; a search for five days using all means possible. We post to numerous lost pet Facebook pages, put up signs at the Post Offices and Community Bulletin Board, and put found dog notices on our local email list, The Town Crier. If no one comes forth to claim a found dog, we are free to re-home them. Toby's dad thanked us and went back into the house. With the boys all mellowed out, I attempted a couple of times to put a collar on the dog but was unsuccessful. I guess he wasn't quite mellow enough. My pointing out that Toby had a beautiful necklace didn't seem to convince him either.

We'd been at it for a while now, and it was clear he wasn't up for wearing a collar any time soon. (I talked to Violet about this story just recently and she remembers it differently. Violet is an animal communicator. She told me she had had a conversation with the dog in which he had agreed to wear a collar. But when I showed up, she said I wanted to do it my way. Which took much longer. I wish I had known she had an agreement! I would have loved to have seen Violet in action and not spent so much time! I had arrived under the impression that she had not been successful at putting a collar on him. She said she just didn't have a large enough collar! We had a good laugh over the miscommunication.)

I decided to go home to get my dog Dinah and see if her presence would help the situation. Dinah is what I refer to as a marshmallow dog; very calm, very gentle, loves everyone and everything and is absolutely non-reactive even to an aggressive dog. She was a shepherd mix of some kind. Dinah had the markings of an Anatolian shepherd but the delicate bones of a Greyhound. She was beautiful. I thought I might be able to slip a collar on the dog while he was busy introducing himself to her. It was certainly worth a try. I told my husband what we were up to, and he said he would help by bringing Dinah down. That was great as I wasn't sure what I would do with two big dogs in one car. While the dog was busy sniffing Dinah, who really liked this new guy and he seemed to like her just as much, I slipped a collar around his neck. He didn't seem fazed. My ploy worked like a charm! As I bent over him to tighten the collar, he reacted! He reared up and turned toward me. I wasn't sure exactly what he was doing, but I was pretty scared! I held my breath. Standing up, he was at least 6 feet tall and weighed as much as I did, possibly more. If he bit me, he would take half my face! I waited what seemed like an eternity, but I knew it was mere seconds. He didn't attack. He dropped down onto all fours and just leaned into me. He didn't fight, he didn't growl, nothing. He just leaned into me. I stood there for a few minutes, just feeling the connection - and his power - as well as the relief that flooded through me. I thanked him for not biting me and told him I was delighted that we could be friends. I stroked him to feel the connection and reassure him that he was safe. I think he knew he was home.

So now what was I going to do with this dog? Despite the connection I felt, I knew I couldn't adopt this guy. I brought him to the house as a temporary foster, and the first thing I said to my husband was: "I have no intention of keeping this dog." We had agreed on no more dogs, and this boy was outside my parameters for adoptable dogs anyway. For me, if a dog is so big that I can't lift him into the car, then he is too big for me to adopt. I also don't like heavy-coated dogs; just too much hair! This dog was both massive and hairy.

I immediately put out a call to the community on our email list, asking if anyone could foster this dog while we were in Italy. No one volunteered. I talked to my pet sitters about having him, in addition to our other pets, asking if they would be OK with one more. They were OK with that, great, huge relief. He really was a lovely dog but big and difficult to contain. We bought him an extra-large crate since I didn't have one large enough for this beast. The very first time in it, he bent the bars in a matter of minutes, and he was out. Clearly, crate training was not in his experience, nor did he want it to be. We bought a heavy-duty crate for him, but we were short on training time. I wanted him to make the kennel his, and that might take some doing. Rather than force him into a crate, he had free range while we would be away. At that moment I was truly grateful I had asked the builders to put in a dog door when we were building the house. It was large and just barely wide enough for this guy to fit through, but he did, and he liked it. I designed a hidden flap in the fence gate that my husband put together. It was high enough that the smaller dogs couldn't access it, but the big dog could come and go as he pleased. He roamed the neighborhood, making friends with just about everyone, including my cat Sabyl. I liked having a big imposing dog on the property. He would be a great guard dog. Big and loud but not aggressive unless he needed to be.

Since he was going to stay for a while, it was time to give the dog a name. He was brilliant. He mastered the dog door in no time, had learned "sit" very quickly as well. Granted he may have known that command already, but who knew? I suggested the name, Einstein. Kind of a lame name I suppose. My husband didn't like it. I said: "OK, how about Albert?" He said: "I like that name, he's Albert then." So, Albert it was. At the end of the week, we took off for Italy, thinking everything would be OK until we returned.

While in Italy we stayed in touch with family back home via Skype. I was grateful to be able to connect so easily, halfway around the globe. While Skyping home partway through the week, my pet sitter, Chris, said Albert was destroying the house. I asked for a definition of "destroying" before I went into full-blown panic.

Albert had managed to shred all of the window screens on the first floor. All but the one in my office, the door was always closed. It would only cost about $50 to replace them all, so that was actually relatively minor. He gouged the woodwork around some doors and on window sills, harder to fix than the screens. We would have to wait until we got home to see how much damage had been done. With dogs, scratches are considered pretty normal wear and tear. It turned not to be such a big deal after all. I was relieved since he was certainly capable of doing real damage. He didn't really destroy much, but it had Chris upset as we had just built the house. After talking a little longer, Chris admitted that he had locked Albert in and the dog just wanted out. From then on, Albert had an open dog door; there was no more damage to the house.

I was surprised as I relayed the message to my husband that he remained so calm. I had assumed he would be very angry. He didn't seem to care much. The woodwork could be repaired, but that would be expensive. We hadn't even been in the house for two years. Damage this early should have been difficult to accept. It was very odd.

Before we left for the trip, I arranged for Violet to drop Albert at the vet on the Monday of our return to be neutered. Albert was familiar with Violet, and I didn't know anyone else who might be able to handle him. Violet was happy to help. I would pick Albert up in the afternoon on Tuesday after I got some rest. Long flights knocked me on my rear for a few days. Violet had him in on schedule; his neuter went well. We returned late that Monday night so the timing was perfect. If possible, I like to leave any animal at the veterinarian for the night after their surgery. This gives the clinic a chance to look for post-surgical issues like bleeding and infection.

I planned to check with the clinic when I got up to be sure Albert was ready to come home. First thing Tuesday morning the phone rang. It was the vet clinic. "How soon can you get here?" they asked. "Oh, no. What happened?" I inquired with dread. "Your dog broke out of the clinic. We cannot open the parking lot gate for fear he will take off, and we have other clients that need to come in!" they told me. "I'll throw on some clothes and be there in 30 minutes!!" I replied in a panic! I was exhausted and severely jet-lagged, but I was suddenly wide awake! I beat it down to the vet clinic as fast as legally possible and arrived to find Albert sitting in the front seat of some guy's truck. Apparently, this other client dropped his dog off then came back out to go home. When he opened his truck door, Albert, still loose in the parking lot, decided he wanted to go for a ride! The man was kind enough to wait for me to arrive before setting Albert free. I was so embarrassed, but at least with Albert contained, they were able to open the clinic! When we opened the cab door, I asked Albert what he thought he was doing. He just cocked his head and gave me a look that said, "What do you mean?! I thought we were going for a ride!" "We are going for a ride, but in MY car," I told him. I leashed Albert and thanked the man for his help and patience then went in to pay the bill.

"How did Albert break out?" I asked. "I'll show you!" Doc said. (I may have groaned.) The recovery or holding kennels have concrete block walls and large, heavy steel doors of vertical bars. They showed me that the doors are removable, but you have to pick them up from the top or bottom and slide them out of their hinges. Albert managed to do this all by himself? I looked at the door and tried to figure out how! Had he gotten his head under it and lifted? Did he stand up and lift the top crossbar? Did he really figure it out or was it dumb luck that he managed it? Albert wasn't telling, but he did seem proud of himself. I thought, "We gave him the perfect name." After removing the steel door to the kennel, he then proceeded to break down the back door. Apparently, he hit it at a run and broke the hinges off! He ripped the door clean off, wow. I offered to pay for a new back door, but the clinic refused. Doc said, "That's just part of running a clinic." Um, really? I know better than to argue with Doc. They did replace the door with a stronger one; I checked it on the next visit. Hopefully, it would be Albert-proof!

Still scratching my head over how he managed his Houdini trick, I took Albert home. I filled my husband in on what had transpired. I posed the question; whether Albert knew what he was doing when he removed the door of the kennel? He thought it was clear Albert knew precisely what he was doing when he broke down the back door. But the holding pen door may have been dumb luck. Either way, it was a funny story we could tell. His surgery went well, so we were ready for Albert to heal and settle into his new life with us until we could find a new home for him. A couple of days later, I noticed scrotal swelling and called the vet. I usually have female dogs but had seen enough neuters in my time to think this was not normal. They said some swelling is perfectly normal. I said this was not typical swelling. A lot of redness or heat indicates infection, as can swelling and oozing. They said to give it a couple of days and let them know how he's doing. I persisted; Albert's scrotum had enlarged to the size of a grapefruit! They still insisted it was "normal." Frustrated, I hung up, mumbling: "It is NOT normal." The next morning when I came down to start the day, there was blood splattering the walls of the living room. Albert was nowhere to be found. I was very concerned. If he had gone out during the night, a pack of coyotes could have attacked after smelling the blood. A single coyote was no match for this guy, but a pack could kill him. I ran outside, calling his name. I couldn't find him. When I came back in to get my husband to help search, Albert was standing in the living room. He had only gone as far as the fenced yard, smart dog! I needed to do a quick assessment to see from where the blood was coming. It was instantly obvious. And, just what I expected. His scrotum had virtually exploded! The swelling was, as I suspected, an abscess, and it ruptured; big time. He had blood all down his hind legs. I immediately called the vet to get him back in. Albert wasn't an old dog; we guessed he was about 18 months old. An older dog, being neutered later in life, is at higher risk for scrotal infection. But, it can happen at any age. Poor guy. So I took him back to the vet for ablation (removal) and in a few days, all would well. Just to be safe, I didn't leave him overnight this time.

While we were in Italy, I had received a couple of inquiries about adopting Albert. I had posted his availability on The Town Crier before we left and I had a couple of suitable prospective adopters. I told my husband that I had people who would like to come and meet Albert and possibly adopt him. I needed to know what time would work for him. He said, "I kind of like him, I'd like to keep him." And so we added another dog. I didn't bring up the fact that we had agreed that we would not adopt any more dogs. I wasn't sure he'd see the inconsistency that left me feeling powerless. If I wanted a dog, the answer was we had too many. If he wanted to keep one, that was OK? I felt I had no voice in the marriage and had been feeling this way for some time. Adding another dog was fine with me, so not the hill to die on. Albert would stay and bring our pack to nine.

A week or so after we adopted Albert I received an email from a friend who said he was a vicious dog. She informed me that he had come from Pilar, a community just north of Dixon and that he would bite people walking down the street. She had been nipped at and growled at on numerous occasions by "him." She also said she saw him in a car a few days after we had adopted him. I told her Albert had not been in a car that day. He was home with me. We later heard that there had been a litter of these dogs in the Pilar area. Albert had a twin, or two. I don't know if the dog in the car was the same one as the dog from Pilar, but it wasn't Albert. He was a pretty mellow dog, didn't demand a lot of attention, liked the other dogs, big and small, and was fine with cats. Growl and bite? It didn't sound at all like Albert, but it is hard to know if in a new home where he feels connected and loved was his behavior different? He was free to come and go, well-fed, groomed, hugged and generally pampered. Had he previously been in an abusive home? Or simply neglected? I had no way of knowing. (Violet may have known, but I never got his story if she did). But the dog I knew showed no signs of aggression. If it was the same dog, he no longer felt the need to nip and growl. Albert was home.

I had my challenges with this guy. He liked to run out to the main road, highway 75. I was OK with Albert out on our arroyo but not on 75. The risk of getting hit was very high. My little French bulldog Cecelia would run with him. Right into traffic! Twice I thought I was going to watch her get killed. Don't for a second imagine a Frenchie can't run fast. This little chunk of a dog was like lightning! Faster than Albert. Each time I had to run down to collect her. Both times she was grinning like a fool. "That was fun!" For her, it may have been "fun." Not for me. After the second time she took off running with Albert was the last time she had the run of the property. After that, she was confined to the fenced yard. She seemed to value her freedom more than her life. I didn't. Before Albert, Cecelia never left the property. She always stayed close to me. Once Cecelia was confined, Albert spent more time next door. The new neighbors were dog people and took an immediate liking to Albert. He was great with their dogs, so he spent many an afternoon romping with them.

Once Albert healed, he was ready to hike and explore with the Tuesday morning hiking group. He did tend to hike on his own terms, but was pretty consistent with recall. He and Turnip soon became regulars with the group.

Boo and Albert became best buddies. He was often next door playing with her and Trooper. And Pete's family loved Albert like one of their own. With his newfound life and friends, he didn't run off to Toby's anymore. I felt a little sad for Toby. He liked his big buddy. I bet he missed him.

Running Free
by sayia willows

As I run I feel free
I feel the wind in my fur
I feel what no one else can feel
The freedom of being a wolf
Free to roam where I want
I feel free being one with the out side the darkness . . .

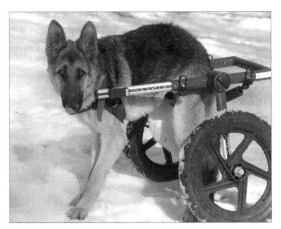

Photo by Judy Pearson

Danaka

This particular experience, I say experience because it wasn't a rescue, It was more a story of connections. This is something I have observed throughout my life, where I happened to be in the right place at the right time. Years ago, I was standing in line at the grocery store in Rhode Island; two women in front of me were talking about their dogs. Of course, I was eavesdropping! One of the women was having to make the difficult decision to euthanize her dog because they couldn't figure out what was wrong, and the dog was dying a slow, painful death. I was grateful that the friend asked what was going on, and as I listened to the symptoms, I knew exactly what they needed to do to save the dog. This was a time before cell phones, so I asked her to promise me that she would go right home and call her vet to do some more blood work. I told her they needed a specific test for pancreatic enzymes. "Are you a vet?" she asked. "No, but I have heard this same story from a friend of mine," I replied. I then told them both that a special diet and enzymes should have the dog back to health quickly. Just being in the right place at the right time.

Of all the stories, this is the one that I think would make a fantastic movie. Not a Hallmark though as it doesn't have a happy ending. It might be the only rescue in this book that doesn't. Still, it's a beautiful story in so many ways.

I first met Laura when she needed dog food. She had numerous dogs, but didn't work a full-time job, so didn't have a lot of money to keep the pack fed. This is a fairly common scenario out here in rural New Mexico. For the past few years, we had received donated dog food through the Wildlife Center in Española. For years Walmart had been donating torn bag pet foods, returned or damaged toys, etc. to the Wildlife Center and other non-profits who could use them.

After a couple of years of working through the Wildlife Center, DAPS got on the direct donation list. We would get the call from Walmart, and had until 3:00 that afternoon to pick up the load. Sometimes if Adele and her truck weren't available, or I wasn't, we had to pass it on to another non-profit. Usually, I could manage to find a volunteer to run down for us. For some volunteers, a dog food pickup is a perfect way to be involved and feel like they were making a difference. They were, and we so appreciated them! But then the donations ceased. It was a sad day for the dogs who depended on donated food and for us. We do still get a few donations from a local pet store, PetSense, for which we are genuinely grateful, but it isn't nearly the volume we could really use.

When the donations were still coming in, we'd load up the bed and park it at a central location in Dixon; the Co-op, Fire Station, Community Center, etc. and hand out the food to those in need. Some people were kind enough to make a small donation to DAPS when they received free food. For some, that was not possible, and they would help unload the bags instead. Very few just came for a handout. If they did, it was because they really needed it. We would store several bags in my little horse trailer for emergencies. Or, for people who couldn't make it to the donation days, to come and pick up later.

Laura lived up on the Taos Mesa and was not able to make it down for donation day so she would call when they were desperate for dog food. Up on the Mesa, there's a community of people who want to live outside society. Some have mental health issues, some are very poor, others work odd jobs to keep going, and some just want out of societal restrictions. They don't have much, but they seem to work together to survive. They live outside the rules, in old buses, campers, makeshift homes. (There are a book and film "On the Mesa" you could read or watch to get a real sense of life on the Mesa.) But briefly the Mesa is an area west of Taos, and it is pretty barren. Mesa means "table" in Spanish. The Taos Mesa is a community. It is hard living out there on flat land. No utilities, no water, anything they need they have to truck out from town. One day when the phone rang, it was Laura who was in an absolute panic. She said that one of their dogs had been shot.

Unfortunately, that does happen here in rural New Mexico. County ordinances allow the shooting of nuisance dogs. After several phone calls to our local vets, all were on overload, we rushed the dog into the only Veterinary Clinic that could take an emergency that morning, Valley Vet in Pojoaque. Upon examination, we found it was not a gunshot wound but a dog bite from a neighbor's dog. Happy news, as that was much easier to treat. Some antibiotics and a few stitches and the dog would be fine. A gunshot wound would, of course, require surgery to remove the bullet and possibly some reconstruction of bone, muscle, or connective tissue, so we got off easy that day.

I didn't really know Laura's living situation, but it sounded like she had a house. She had dogs that didn't necessarily get along, with each other or the neighbor's dogs, so she needed to put up fencing. I happened to have some leftover fencing from our DAPS kennel project, so she came down and picked it up. I hoped this would mean fewer dog fights and calls for medical assistance. I have foster kennels on my property. One free-standing, one off the back of the house and a kennel off my ceramic and glass studio. There the dogs have an inside room and a fully fenced outside run.

I put a potbelly wood stove in the studio kennel so that I didn't have to run electric heaters in the winter to keep the dogs warm. Heating with wood is much more economical. I like it better too, it just feels and smells cozy. I'm not sure the dogs had an opinion. As long as it was warm enough, they were happy. It was a few weeks later that Laura called me to tell me about her friend Cindy and her situation. Good thing she wasn't calling about another incident with her dogs as she had reached our limit on Vet care. We do as much as we can for as many as we can. But at some point, we have to say no. In this case, there had been numerous emergencies with her dogs, so we were tapped out. Laura hadn't called about her dogs, they were doing fine. She'd called to see if DAPS could help Cindy with a wheelchair for her young German shepherd Dog. I told her that I didn't think we had the resources, but I would see what I could do. After hearing Cindy's story, I was pretty much hell-bent on finding her one.

Cindy and her husband Dave also lived up on the Mesa, and were friends with Laura. Dave was a good mechanic and was always rebuilding a truck or two. Around here that's a valuable skill. We don't have any emissions testing, so a lot of people drive vehicles that are 30 or 40 years old, or more, and need constant maintenance. Like many on the Mesa Cindy and Dave were poor, but they managed to get by. They were in their 40s and had been together forever. They loved each other very much, loved their children (now grown), loved their dogs. They had the kind of relationship many of us dream about. True love if you will. They didn't have much if you are talking about material things, but they had each other; that was all that really mattered. Cindy was an excellent cook, and Dave didn't miss a meal. One afternoon Dave had been out working on a truck. He knew when to be in for dinner.

When her husband didn't come in to eat, Cindy became concerned. Dave never missed a meal. If he was deep into a project, he might be a little late, but that night he was really off the schedule. Cindy went to check on him to see what was holding him up. When she rounded the corner to the garage, she saw him under the truck, and she knew Dave was dead. The front axle on the pickup truck had fallen on him, crushing his chest. He had died there pinned under the pickup. In shock, she went back to the house to call 911.

The next few days were a blur of activity and final decisions. Cindy had Dave cremated. She'd scatter his ashes in a favorite spot when she was ready. There was a small family gathering with a few close friends at the local church. Devastated, Cindy didn't know how she would go on without Dave. The community rallied to do what they could to help her but going on without her beloved husband seemed pointless. Cindy brought Dave's ashes home and together with his dog Beau, a pit bull, scattered Dave's ashes under the tree where he and Beau liked to sit and have a cold drink and an afternoon nap to escape the hot summer sun. A man and his best friend in the shade of the tree. Cindy would keep that image in her mind for years to come.

After Dave's death, Cindy would find Beau under the tree every day. Beau seemed to be waiting for Dave to arrive for their daily nap in the shade of the old tree. On the eighth day after the funeral, Cindy watched Beau curl up under the tree as he had every day. It was a sweet sight. But on this afternoon Beau never got up. Evening was starting to fall, and it was time for Beau to come in. When he didn't show, Cindy went out to see why Beau was staying out so late. She could see that he was still asleep under the tree. As Cindy approached, she called his name, but the dog didn't respond. Cindy wondered if he was going deaf. She knelt down to gently nudge him awake, but he didn't wake up; she could feel that he was cold, too cold. Beau also had died. There had been no indication of any health issues, he was a young, healthy dog. Cindy looked for signs of distress like gastric torsion (commonly known as bloat) or poisoning. There was plenty of antifreeze and other car fluids that dogs like, but are deadly if ingested, around the garage but those too would cause distress. Beau had apparently just gone to sleep. Cindy believed he died of a broken heart. He so loved Dave that he just couldn't live without him.

Cindy understood that the bond between the two had been profound, as deep as any dog and master could be. It was another devastating loss for Cindy. Losing them both in such a short time was almost unbearable. Friends also now grieved both Dave and his dog Beau. Once again, they did what they could to support Cindy. One friend, who bred German shepherd dogs, gave Cindy a puppy with the thought that it would help her with the loss of her husband and his beloved dog. A sweet puppy to help her heal, what a beautiful gift! Cindy fell in love! She named the puppy Danaka and took her everywhere. It was precisely what Cindy needed, a puppy couldn't change what happened with Dave and Beau, but the love of a beautiful German shepherd puppy would help her go on.

At first, Danaka was a typical rambunctious pup, but, after a couple of months, Cindy noticed that Danaka wasn't gaining weight, growing, but she was getting thinner. Dani had a healthy appetite, yet she wasn't gaining anything. In another month, Danaka had started to walk oddly, stumbling, and losing her balance. Thinking maybe she had injured herself, pulled a muscle, sprained a knee or ankle, or had a hip issue as many German shepherds do, Cindy took her to the vet. She paid for numerous tests, and the bill was growing. This woman with little income was willing to do or spend everything to save her beautiful puppy. The veterinarian couldn't find anything definitively wrong with Danaka so they sent her home with some pain meds thinking maybe she indeed just pulled a muscle or had some other soft tissue injury, something minor that would resolve shortly with some rest. It didn't. Desperate to find what was wrong, Cindy took Dani to three different vet clinics. All took x-rays, did thorough exams, ran tests, but no one could figure out why Danaka was losing the use of her hind legs. Her issue didn't appear to be neurological. It didn't seem to be physical either. By the age of about four months, Danaka was unable to walk. She dragged herself around, rear legs useless. Her front legs were strong, but dragging her back end like that was going to cause injury if it continued. Cindy was resourceful and simply wrapped a towel around Danaka's hips, creating a makeshift harness. Cindy walked Danaka around so she could build strength and go potty.

This was the perfect solution for a while, but as Danaka continued to grow, it started to be a problem for Cindy.

She wasn't very tall, so holding Danaka up high enough was no longer physically possible. She was exhausted and in pain. That's when Laura called me to see if we could purchase a wheelchair for Danaka. It was one of those times when DAPS had almost no money, so buying anything was out of the question. But there had to be a way to help this sweet woman and her pup. I thought I'd look on Craigslist or eBay to get a sense of what a dog wheelchair for a medium-sized dog would cost. Perhaps Laura and Cindy, or we, could raise funds needed. I didn't know if that would be possible but had to do something. I thought somehow something would come up so we could help this little dog. Cindy had been through too much already, I had to find a way.

I searched eBay to see how expensive a dog wheelchair was and if I could find one used that was affordable. Most were far outside our budget unless we raised a few hundred dollars fast. I was thinking it wasn't going to happen when I saw a listing for a dog wheelchair that had been reconfigured to fit a smaller German shepherd. Wow! Danaka is a more petite German shepherd! It might be just her size! It was listed for $150. We could raise that kind of money pretty quickly, but someone would have to have the time to do it; I wasn't that someone. We had a Board of Directors who were enthusiastic and often helped with events and clinics, but I doubted anyone had time to fundraise. It was too much work, and we all had full, busy lives. Besides, this needed to happen quickly if we were to save this dog, so there was no time to pull together an event that would generate enough funds.

My initial enthusiasm was fading fast. No time, no funds, no help, I was feeling defeated. With nothing to lose, I thought I'd send the owner a message asking if he would be willing to donate it to DAPS for a dog in need. If not, perhaps he'd lower his price for us? Anything would help. We could offer him a tax deduction for the donation if that persuaded him. If he said no, then we'd find another way to get one. But I'd never know if I didn't try! I sent the seller a message through eBay explaining Danaka's situation and who DAPS was. I asked if he was in a position to make a donation and let him know we understood if that was not possible. I didn't expect to hear a reply at all as I waited with my heart in my throat. Not only did he reply almost immediately, but he also responded with "Of course I would!" Through tears of gratitude, I wrote to him that DAPS would be very happy to pay the shipping. But to that, he replied, "I'll even pay the shipping." Tears of gratitude were just streaming. This man's generosity had just renewed my faith in human beings! We exchanged phone numbers so we could talk more in depth. In his deep Alabama accented voice he told me his name was Bly. He was a retired Alabama State Trooper. He then told me the story of his dog. How, as his dog aged, like many German shepherds, he lost the use of his hind legs due to hip dysplasia. When he purchased the wheelchair for his dog, it was just too big for him. Bly custom fitted the wheelie by cutting the uprights down short enough that the dog could reach the ground. I could just picture the small dog suspended in the wheelie, legs pumping, but only pumping air. How confused he must have been! Bly said the dog loved his wheelie and it gave him a few more years of mobility. He was an old dog and time finally caught up. Bly's dog had lived a good long life, was a great dog and beloved companion. And from the cracking in Bly's voice, I could tell how deeply he loved him. Bly said he was now too old to think about getting another dog so wouldn't be needing the wheelie.

I tried to convince him otherwise. There are so many older dogs that need loving homes, but the loss was a difficult one, so Bly wasn't inclined. I told him I understood and respected his feelings. I felt like I'd known this man for years. Tough on the outside, great big warm heart on the inside. It was so good that we had made this amazing connection. It had taken Bly a while to bring himself to sell the wheelie. It was the last reminder of his dog. He had just posted it but wasn't sure it would fit any dog since he had customized it. And I never thought we'd find one the right size for our little girl that we could afford and this was the first one I considered!

How's that for meant to be?! I hung up the phone with Bly. Some good people do good things, not for any reward; just because it's the right thing to do. Bly was one of those people, and I was deeply moved by his generosity.

Danaka was still a young dog so she would continue to grow, but I didn't think she would be a large dog. We didn't know how long she had left to live, but we had hoped to figure out what the problem was in time. In the meantime, if she had a wheelchair, she'd have mobility and be able to get some good exercise that might increase her strength and improve her health. It might be just what she needed. In short order, the wheelchair arrived, and I put it together. Laura picked it up and delivered it to Cindy for me. I checked in a couple of days later and learned that Danaka had taken to it instantly! Cindy sent me a video clip of Danaka trying it out for the first time. It didn't take her any time to figure it out and start running around the yard! She was amazing! And I swear she was smiling. I asked Cindy if we could meet in Taos at the park so I could take some video and meet her and Danaka. I wanted to take some photos and talk about Danaka's problems. Seems to me there had to be something the vets were missing. It didn't make any sense for this young girl who ate heartily to still be so thin and losing the use of her hind legs.

We met at Kit Carson Park in the center of Taos. The park had numerous areas; two large open fields where they held concerts and events, a kids' playground with all the swings and climbing apparatus any kid could want, and a dog park. We chose one of the open fields as it had plenty of room to run without the distraction of other dogs and was close to the street so accessible and easy to locate. I figured I'd recognize Dananka instantly even if I didn't know Cindy. I saw the dog first, and it was apparent by the joy on her face, who her mom was! When I met Danaka, I could see her brightness; a happy, exuberant dog. She was so sweet she gave me kisses! I wondered if she was thanking me. She was a pro at the wheelchair. It was late winter when we met, so the park still had snow and some mud, but she managed all of it with ease and joy. It didn't hurt that the wheelie had all terrain tires! She just seemed so happy to have the freedom to move, and move she did! What a beautiful girl. We watched her run around for another 15 minutes at which time she appeared to be getting tired. I didn't want to stress her already fragile body. We loaded her in the car, Cindy and I hugged, Dananka gave me a few more sweet kisses and off they went. I wondered if I would ever see her again.

It was abundantly clear that something was very wrong. Danaka was too thin, too small, too weak. But what was it? I heard from Laura a few months later that Danaka was again close to death. More tests were run, and still, the vets could not figure out what was wrong with her, but she rallied once again, at least for a while. During my conversation with Laura this morning, I learned that Danaka had finally passed. Laura described to me how Danaka's food would stick to her teeth and stick in her throat. Cindy would have to save her from choking, and finally one day, she could not clear the obstruction, and Danaka choked to death. With this information, I now think that Danaka had some kind of enzyme deficiency like Glycogen Storage Disease Type III (curious that the acronym for German shepherd dog And Glycogen Storage Disease are the same- GSD) or perhaps a salivary deficiency as well. Most animals and humans start digesting food in our mouth. Without the proper enzymes and salivary output, her food would stick in her mouth and throat. Danaka also wasn't able to break down her food and absorb enough the nutrients to survive. GSD is a very rare disorder and difficult to diagnose; impossible to treat beyond crisis episodes of low blood sugar. Though it was not a treatable disease, it's one of those times that I wish I had known more and so wish I could've done more. My heart just ached for Cindy. Having met her and seen what a strong woman she is, I know she'll be fine, eventually, despite having suffered so many painful losses in such a short amount of time.

Cindy did get another dog once she had some healing time. She had put so much into trying to save Danaka that she was exhausted both mentally and physically. The last time I checked in Cindy and the dog were doing well. I met up with her in Taos to deliver some dog food for the new pup. She was with a carload of kids, grandkids, and dogs. All were happy and seemed to be past the pain of the loss. I offered to pay for a spay for the newest member of the canine family; it was the least we could do for this incredible woman considering all she had endured. I hugged her and said goodbye.

A Dog Sits Waiting
by Jinx Natta

A dog sits waiting,
Her plumes tail gently waving,
As she waits for you to return.
She thought that they were going to get out to play,

Too faithful to walk away,
The dog stays waiting,
Day after day . . .

Photo by Judy Pearson

Tui

They were like radar. I had never seen ears on a dog like those on Tui!! Sticking out a full six inches off her head! She had to be part Chihuahua with ears like those. Why was she here and who was responsible? That is a question that is generally without an answer.

Word arrived, both by phone and in-person while in town that two Chihuahua mixes had been dumped on highway 75 on the way to Peñasco. "Did you see those two Chihuahuas?" Tommy asked when I ran into him at the Co-op. "No, where are they?" I asked. "Just past your road on the way to Peñasco." He filled me in. I said I had not been up that way in quite a while, so not surprised I hadn't seen them. Jeannie was also receiving phone calls with questions about what could be done about the Chihuahuas. Numerous people had seen the dogs sitting right on the highway and were concerned they would be hit.

Highway 75 is a two-lane road with no shoulder to speak of and no breakdown lane. It either drops into a ditch or just continues out into scrub sage, a bit of grass and sandstone hills that glow golden in the early morning and late afternoon light. It's a narrow rural highway, but it's the main drag through town; it gets a lot of use. These two girls were just feet from traffic, so people were justifiably concerned about their safety. The dogs had chosen a spot near a sizable drainage culvert that would allow them to cross under the highway safely. They were on the west side, probably where they were dumped, which offered little protection. Each time we have had a dumped dog, they have stayed in the area where they were left. I'm sure they wait there for their owner to return, not understanding that they will not. I suppose they have no way of comprehending what has just happened to them. Hachiko, the Japanese Akita, who waited at the train station for his owner to return for nine years (his owner died) is an example in the extreme. This behavior is attributed to the "loyalty" of the dog, but it may be something we really don't understand. Abandoned dogs, like these girls, are often not well cared for and/or show signs of abuse, and yet, they wait for their owner to return. Sometimes for a very long time.

Jeannie and I talked to compare the information we had each received. The dogs were both quite skittish. No one could get close enough to get a collar or leash on them, so they had been on the highway for a couple of days before I learned of their situation and location. Jennie filled me in saying there were a couple of local people who had been feeding the dogs for the past few days. One of our locals, Tommy, has a great big heart and helps in every way he can when he sees a dog in need. He had gone up the road to feed them every day so that they wouldn't starve.

Immediately after hanging up the phone, I hopped in the truck and drove up the street looking for two tiny dogs. Sure enough, there they were right by the culvert, but they weren't tiny! They were sitting right next to the highway, curled up together. They appeared to be mother and daughter. I didn't get very close before the younger one got up to movemfarther away, looking absolutely petrified. As she got up, I could see her round, full belly. By the fullness, I assumed she was pregnant. I've seen a case of worms nearly that full, but I didn't think it was worms this time. I wasn't convinced they were Chihuahua mixes, they were too big. The younger dog, probably just a puppy, had giant ears that stuck up and out. She was adorable though pretty funny looking too. She was long and low, tan with a pinkish brown nose and dark muzzle with beautiful brown mascara lined eyes of gold. I suspected she was actually a Corgi mix. Being part Corgi certainly would account for those ears! Her mom was similar, only smaller, shorter and darker, without the radar ears. She had prick ears, but hers were far more proportionate and more Corgi-like. With their respective ages, it made sense that they were mother and daughter. Both resembled some kind of sausage. At least they were well fed. It was hard to tell, but it appeared that momma might also be pregnant. We often get dogs that are dumped because they are "pregnant again." These two were so bonded that I hated to separate them. Could I possibly keep them together? If they had large litters, I just didn't have space. I'd figure it out one way or another.

Right now, I had to focus on catching these girls and taking them home. I looked around and had to laugh when I saw what people have been feeding them! Cheese puffs, leftover shrimp scampi, and Vienna sausage. I wasn't really surprised that it was all still lying on the ground. The dogs just didn't seem to be interested in eating any of it. Smart girls! I wouldn't eat it either. I knew Tommy had been leaving regular dog food for them, so it wasn't a concern. They were both so chubby that a couple of missed meals would not hurt them one bit. I so appreciated the effort by the community and their concern for these girls. I imagined a local driving home with leftovers and seeing the dogs by the side of the road, cold, alone, and hungry. They cared enough to give up the food they had bothered to bring home for another day. The thoughtfulness and personal sacrifice warmed my heart and made me smile.

I headed back to the DAPS-Mobile to collect the items I needed to try to catch the dogs. As I was gathering my crate, collars, leashes and dog treats, out of the truck, a car pulled over on the opposite side of the highway right where the two dogs were curled up. It was two women I knew pretty well. Both were animal lovers and rescuers. One was suffering from Rheumatoid Arthritis, a debilitating disease, but was determined to keep her animals and help as much as she could. The other was terrific with animals and worked as a dog trainer. I was happy to see them both, and to have their help. They had seen the dogs on the road earlier and had stopped on their way back through with their own supplies to try to catch them. I was able to get close to the mom and get a leash around her neck, but she was so scared that I couldn't get her to walk with me. She just sat there, unmoving. Rather than frighten her further, we corralled her into the crate by forming a barrier with cardboard. She was quickly funneled into the container with no means of escape. She seemed quite happy to be there too! Dogs often feel safe in a crate, especially if they have been crate trained. We had no idea if she had been trained or not, but she was calm and quiet in the soft enclosure.

When we crated the momma dog, the younger one took off. She was very skittish and clearly frightened. This always makes me wonder how she had been treated. Being dumped is a good indication of the lack of care for this sweet girl, but beyond that, it would take time for other issues to become apparent. After a futile attempt to coax her over with yummy treats and happy talk, I had to give up for the time being and drove the mom to the shelter in Taos.

I talked to and petted the mom all the way to the Shelter. She seemed sweet but pretty shut down. Often that indicates abuse and/ or neglect. Heartbreaking to see a dog so frightened. It was a bit encouraging that she seemed to like the stroking I was giving her. I couldn't get my entire hand in the crate without risking her escape, so she was just getting little two-finger strokes on her head. She showed no aggression toward me, which made me hopeful. During her intake, I explained the situation and what I feared, that she too was pregnant. She was very, very shy, but sweet. With time and attention, she might come around; that was always an unknown. These dogs clearly had not had a lot of human contact and were possibly abused. Same old story gets really tiring, and really old, really fast.

I called the shelter the next day to see how she was doing. During her intake exam, they found that she was indeed spayed so just chubby, not pregnant. That was a huge relief. Lucky for her, there were volunteers at the shelter willing to work with her to try to socialize her. They found that when it was one particular person who worked with her regularly, she started to open up and bond, but it took time and patience. Hers was going to be a difficult adoption. She was given the name Mitzi. I checked in over the next few weeks to see how Mitzi was doing and receive updates both on behaviors that might be problematic and positive improvement. After a couple of months of working with her, the volunteer who named her adopted her! Theirs was a special bond, and no one believed she would bond with anyone else. I understand how that is. My Turnip is a similar case.

In the meantime, this younger dog, who I named "Tui" after a character in the television series *Top of the Lake*, was out in the wild and in considerable danger. Young and pregnant, she ran off into the hills to have the baby on her own. In the case of feral, or semi-feral dogs like Tui, the sire can be almost any dog within a few miles, including a related male. Like the show, Tui was a teen, in dog years, and possibly pregnant by her father, and now on her own in the hills. With litters like Tui's, where the mother dog is outside and unprotected, there are often as many fathers as there are puppies. We see some amazingly varied litters because of it. Tui was young so her litter would likely be small. At least I hoped so!

We knew we had a mountain lion that passed through the area where Tui was hiding. We had recently lost a couple of neighborhood dogs to mountain lion attacks, so I didn't hold out a lot of hope for this cute, scared, little momma dog. She was no match for a mountain lion. The terrain was hilly, covered in scrub brush and wild grass. Not much protection anywhere. I went out twice a day, for the first two days, and left food for her with the hope of gaining her confidence; I couldn't find her. Once I spotted her far off in the hills, but she wasn't coming close anytime soon. Each time I put food out it was gone when I returned. I hoped it was Tui who was eating it. She needed the nourishment with a belly full of puppies. She was so afraid, and that was not going to change quickly or easily. I could not get near her, and she would not approach. The longer she was out alone, the higher the chance she'd be attacked. Or, if she survived, the higher the chance she'd have the puppies in the wild. In that case, they would probably be eaten by the mountain lion or coyotes. It wasn't looking good.

It was February so the nights were still pretty cold and we were heading into a cold snap. Freezing and exposure would make survival even less likely, so trapping was becoming critical.

I set the trap; placed it away from the road, back behind some shrubbery and a mountain of dirt. I baited the trap with some smelly canned food that would hopefully waft on the breeze and bring Tui in. I had no idea how long it might take or if it would work at all, but I had to give it a shot. I decided to check the trap regularly over the next few hours as the sun was setting and it would soon be dark. I didn't want Tui in the trap for too long out in the cold. An hour later I decided to go check on it. I didn't think an hour was anywhere near long enough, and I'm not really sure why I checked on it that soon; it just seemed like I should. To my absolute surprise and delight, I returned to find her in the trap! That was the quickest trapping I'd ever done. She was clearly hungry after being out for a couple of nights. I approached the trap with caution. I didn't want to frighten her anymore than she already was. I approached slowly, talking in that dog trainer/rescuer happy voice. I was ready for her to snap, bark, growl, or fight to escape. She didn't do any of that. Instead, she sat perfectly still, just looking at me. This was an excellent sign! I was so relieved and felt the tension leave my body. She clearly was not aggressive, not in the least. I felt sure enough that I stuck my fingers through the side of the trap and stroked her. She just looked at me with her beautiful mascara lined eyes. I couldn't read her yet, but she was calm and didn't seem terribly afraid. Nor was she resigned. It felt like she knew she needed to allow this so that she could be safe. I assured her that it would get better from here and hoped she believed me.

Tui was small enough that I could pick the trap up and slide it into the back of the truck without assistance. I opened the sliding glass window between the cab and the bed so I could talk to her and listen to her as we headed home. Once back, I put her in the studio kennel with the older dogs because they were very dog-friendly and mellow. I figured Tui would be happy to have some company. They accepted her without issue. I was able to put a collar on her without any resistance. That was another good sign. Some dogs will fight the collar or leash when they have not worn either previously or, if they have been chained. Tui may have once had a collar, or it was just not uncomfortable for her to wear, I had no way of knowing, but she didn't resist. I gave her lots of treats, and it was clear I would gain her confidence very quickly. She was such a sweet, funny little dog.

I called one of our vets, Taos Vet, to schedule a full check-up and first shots. I also wanted to see precisely how pregnant she was. In my experience, once cats and dogs are visibly pregnant, it's only a couple of weeks before they deliver. Neither Jeannie nor I can bring ourselves to do a late-term spay, so I needed to know where Tui was in her gestation. Again, since she appeared pregnant, I assumed we were already too late. On the ride up she sat in the passenger seat with her head in my lap. We were bonding quickly. Tui clearly had never been to the Vet, nuzzling into my lap while we waited. The poor girl was petrified; afraid of just about everything! It was all strange and new. I did what I could to keep her calm and reassure her that it all was OK. We were taken to an exam room, and I sat cuddling Tui on the floor as we waited for Dr. Jeff. Dr. Jeff, at Taos Vet, is very good at palpating a dog's belly and knowing when she is due. Tui was scared but sat for the "belly bop" as he calls it. I watched his hands and Tui's eyes. Her concern was written all over her face, fear in her eyes, but she did it! He gently bounced her belly with his fingers to feel the heads of the puppies. The relative size gives him an idea of how far along they are. He can also guess how many puppies she is carrying. He couldn't offer an exact number, but Tui would not have a large litter. I was so grateful to hear that! Dr. Jeff estimated that she would give birth in two weeks. That was far too late for us to spay. By law if I asked him to, he was required to terminate the pregnancy. Jeannie and I had discussed it before the appointment, and neither of us could terminate this late. At two weeks out the puppies are almost viable, they're fully formed, but their lungs and digestive tract need the last two weeks to fully develop. These puppies were coming into the world! Dr. Jeff was relieved to hear this because he, like most vets, does not like to do late-term spays.

We would schedule a transfer to Colorado when the puppies were old enough, eight to ten weeks, depending on the mother's behavior. Most start to wean at around six weeks. Some will reject their puppies earlier, and we have to step in if that's the case. Most momma dogs will let the puppies nurse the full six to eight weeks. We give them a couple more weeks to socialize, gain confidence, and have critical mom time before we send them to new homes. We do adopt locally to good homes, but more often than not litters are sent off to Colorado where the spay and neuter programs have been so successful that they need our puppies. That was all down the road a bit, so we headed back home to prepare for the arrival of puppies.

I introduced Tui to the indoor dogs, the "Littles," so that she could be in the house close to the guest bathroom, a.k.a. The Whelping room. The Littles are generally accommodating, but I wasn't sure how Tui would be with the three of them. I introduced them one at a time so she wouldn't be overwhelmed. She couldn't have been more underwhelmed! She was okay with the Littles, acted like she didn't really care about them at all. Not scared, not aggressive, genuinely indifferent to the three of them. She was the same with the cats. I'm not sure I'd seen a dog so disinterested in fellow four-legged friends. It was all good, and that was all that mattered. She needed to feel safe when she had the puppies. The Littles accepted her right into their pack. She hopped up on the sofa and made herself at home.

Exactly 2 weeks later, Tui went into labor. Dr. Jeff had nailed it! Two weeks to the day. I had set up the bathtub with cushions and towels, everything to make her comfy while she whelped. She jumped into the tub and started the nesting behavior that indicates whelping is imminent. She circled around, fluffing the pillows and rearranging them, so she was comfortable. It was funny to watch. She'd make a pile and lie down. Just seconds later she was up again rearranging, then she'd lie down. Within a few seconds, up again. She just couldn't get comfortable. I figured it was the size of her belly and the activity of the puppies as they changed position to enter the birth canal and come into the world. This went on for five minutes or so before I decided it might go on for a very long time, so I left. Nesting can begin hours before labor actually commences. Every few minutes, I went back to check-in. As I was watching her, wondering how long it would take, the first contraction hit.

Tui let out a scream! A blood-curdling horror movie scream! I wasn't prepared for that! She clearly wasn't ready for any of it. I jumped up to be right by her in case something was really wrong. She looked at me as her entire body contracted. It was a look that said, "What is happening to me?!" My thought was that this must be her first litter, she was quite young, and she didn't seem to understand what was happening. With another contraction and just a whimper, the first puppy arrived. Tui was clearly confused, looking from me to the puppy and back again. Her expression saying, "What is that?!" She just left the tiny puppy on the pillow, still in its sac, and just looked at it. She showed no signs of comprehension that it was a puppy or of what to do for it. I wasn't sure how long the pup could stay there before we lost it, so I stepped in. I tore open the sac, watched it take its first breath, and presented her with the wiggly puppy. At that moment her maternal instincts kicked in and she took over. I just sat back and watched her and stroked her to reassure her that all was well. She was a good momma! She gently pulled the sac from the pup with her front teeth, ate it and the placenta, and licked the puppy clean.

I'm sure for some watching this is not easy, it's kind of gross. It's bloody. It's messy. The mother eats the sac and afterbirth; both are excellent sources of protein and energy for her to continue with the delivery. So, yes, it was messy, but it was also one of the most beautiful events I've ever witnessed. The other puppies came quite close together so within about two hours we were done! We had two adorable little girls and a little boy. All three were tan with black masks and black interspersed from head to toe. They resembled mom but darker. It was tough to guess what the father might have been. Since they all had the same markings I was going with just one dad; shepherd perhaps? It didn't really matter. They were an interesting mix for sure. What mattered was that they were all healthy and strong. They were all feeding within minutes. That was an excellent sign. I left this beautiful family to bond and rest from the ordeal that is whelping.

With all whelping moms they stay in my guest bathroom until the puppies' eyes open, sometimes longer. It really depends on the size of the dogs, the size of the litter, and the weather. In the warm weather, a mother can be in the outdoor kennel during pregnancy through to transfer time. Since the weather was not yet warm enough and both Tui and the litter were relatively small, they would stay in the room for a few weeks. This meant I had to take Tui out to potty regularly. Since she had been an outdoor dog, this proved challenging! Walking on a leash was foreign. Potty training was new, and she didn't want to leave her puppies. At first, she held it for days. I'd return home to find a mess in the bathroom. Without being too graphic, I found a small mountain of poo and a urine lake. Poor girl! To save the floor, I lined the room with plastic sheeting and puppy pads. We were more diligent as we continued with potty training. Tui must have gotten tired of the mess and smell, and one day followed me right out the door! Up until this breakthrough, there were days when I had to carry her out to the dog yard as she refused to go out. If it was raining all bets were off. She was a stubborn little girl. But I assured her I was even more stubborn than she! Had I won? I don't know, but I was grateful that it was no longer a battle of wills. She probably welcomed the break from nursing at this point too. In a short time, she was housebroken. I knew because she'd bark when she needed to go out. This was one smart dog! But I say this about most of the dogs I work with. Not all, but most.

It was amazing to watch how the puppies grew day by day. Since there were only three, there was plenty of milk for all of them and more teats than needed. No one ever went hungry. I handled them daily so they would be socialized right from the get-go. When they were a week old, I took them to the vet for their first check-up. Tui was also due for her next round of shots. She didn't like being at the vet, and she really didn't like immunizations! But she was better than during her first visit. They all got a clean bill of health. They loaded into the soft crate in the front seat, and I headed to the rink. It was our end of season skating show. I left Tui in the car with the windows cracked for fresh air in the soft crate with the puppies. It was a beautiful day, not too cold for them since it was bright and sunny. They had water and each other. It was a great day to nap in the sun. The show wasn't a big production, only about 45 minutes, so I wouldn't be away for long. After the show, we'd head home.

The show went well! We had a great time. A couple of people who knew asked how I managed with my now ex-husband and his girlfriend sharing the ice. I just told them what they did was none of my concern. I had my job to do, and that was my focus period. What else could I do? I told our Show Director that I needed to run out to check on the pups and I'd be back for the post-show celebration. When I got to the car, Tui was in an absolute froth. She was soaking wet! At first, I thought she'd spilled the water, but when I looked at her, she looked frantic! I quickly looked around in the crate to see what could be wrong and saw only two puppies. "Where's the third Tui?!" I asked, my heart pounding and my stomach turning over. I felt sick. Something was very wrong! I got her out of the crate and found the little boy had been suffocated. This is something that happens so often with young mothers. They sit or lie on them without realizing it. I grabbed the lifeless little boy and started CPR and mouth-to-nose resuscitation. To my surprise and relief, he came back! He heaved a big deep breath and started to cry. So did I! I placed them all back in the crate so he could nurse and be with Tui. I ran in, pulled off my skates, and told everyone I couldn't stay as I had a puppy emergency. Still in a panic, I called our emergency vet to see who was on call. It was Dr. Sides, one of the best! She had just gone out to lunch. I said I would meet her at the clinic when she was done. I kept an eye on the little guy and waited. He felt warm, too warm. Since it was February, we still had snow, so I placed the pup on a snowbank to try to cool him down. I was so upset that I'd caused him heat stroke. Dr. Sides arrived quickly; I told her the story that they had been in the car, and mom seemed awfully hot. It was February it couldn't have been too hot in the car it was warm, it was comfortable, it wasn't hot. She reassured me that this wasn't heatstroke. It was a lovely day but nowhere near sunny enough to be a problem. She examined a little guy; when she turned him over, we saw that his belly was covered in bruises. Apparently, he had wiggled off the edge of the seat and gotten stuck. Tui tried to pull him out, and when she couldn't, she panicked. She clawed at him so hard she caused bruising and internal bleeding. He was treated with anti-inflammatories and fluids, and I took him home. We had no way of knowing how badly he was injured or if he would survive. It was going to be a wait-and-see. I kept him in my lap so I could monitor his breathing; on the way home, he had his first seizure. At home, Tui and the three pups and I headed for the bathtub. Tui hopped in, and I placed all three puppies next to her to nurse. I stayed with them all evening. They nursed and slept. Later that evening, the little boy started to pass blood. I called our local Vet here in Dixon, Dr. Kim, and she said she'd come over to check on him.

It was touch and go. I couldn't leave the tiny puppy, not for a minute. We didn't know if he would make it and there wasn't much anyone could do to save him either. The puppies had been feeding with mom in the tub, but the little boy wasn't nursing well. He'd latch on but gave up quickly, like he just didn't have the strength to continue. He appeared to be going in and out of consciousness. While I was on the phone with Dr. Kim, he had a massive seizure and died. I started CPR again, but I couldn't revive him this time. My heart sank. He was only a week old! We had done everything we could; it was just one of those unfortunate accidents.

I gave Tui a few minutes to be with her dead baby hoping she'd understand he was gone. She seemed far less upset about it than I was. I was a mess; it was my fault. I should have done something differently. I let both Vets know the outcome, and they both assured me that it just happens. Moms will roll over not knowing they're on a puppy and the puppy suffocates. Tui unwittingly had injured her puppy. She knew he was in trouble, and she did what she could. Recalling this story isn't easy. It was awful - gut-wrenching - finding that limp, little, week-old puppy was something I hoped to never experience again. I threw away that soft crate. I couldn't stand the sight of it.

Tui seemed to take the loss in stride. At first, she would look for the little boy and then look at me. All I could do was tell her he was gone. The two girls thrived. They were too young to know he was gone or that he even existed.

The girls were almost identical. Thankfully one had white toes, and the other was a polydactyl. She had six toes on her hind feet. I would never have been able to tell them apart otherwise. I dubbed the polydactyl "Polly." The other was named by one of my skating students who had hoped to adopt her. She and her dad came to visit the puppies and choose which puppy they might like. Becca asked, "Well, could my puppy be Tui too?" I told her, of course she could, and we'd call her Tutu for short! I showed Becca photos of Tutu every week. I often took some videos so she could watch her grow. When Tutu was old enough, they'd pick her up and take her home. Unfortunately, Becca's parents separated, so it wasn't time to bring a puppy into the family.

We put the word out when the two were ready for their new homes. Mary, who worked with Jeannie's husband, was looking to adopt and she wanted two girls. She and her adult son, who lived on the same property, would share the responsibility of taking care of the puppies. Bob knew Mary would be a responsible owner, so with that recommendation, it was a done deal. Mary came down to meet the girls and was just instantly in love! She held them up and smothered them with kisses. It was so sweet. We both had tears in our eyes. They had been socialized since the minute they were born. They had had lots of human contact, socialized with other dogs and cats, they were wonderful, beautiful puppies. It was so heartwarming that they went to a great home where they could be together. It is so hard to let them go after bonding so profoundly, they were my first litter after all! But it also felt so good, so rewarding, knowing that someone else would love them just as much. Mary kept the name Polly, but she changed Tutu's name to "Sammy." She uses the same Vet Clinic the girls were with so they would have continued care for the rest of their lives. For a little while, I kept up with them, but at some point, it was time to let them be. I was no longer needed here.

Tui settled in with the pack of Littles and seemed quite content. She wasn't a dog's dog. She didn't really care if the other dogs were there or not. She also did not do well with other people. It took Jeannie six months to gain her confidence! She only wanted to be with me. I have a tough time letting go of these dogs that have been so badly treated, through neglect and abuse. They come in here, and they learn to be part of my family. We bond deeply. I just can't cause another trauma by taking that away from them. I knew I could find Tui a suitable home but hadn't she been through enough? Some people say that's about me. I had 10 dogs here; I didn't need another one. My life would be simpler without them. The ones that are here are souls that need to be here. So Tui was going to stay with me.

Tui and I went for walks, and she learned to be on a leash. Most free-range dogs hate a collar and leash; at first, they fight to break free. I often use a harness as it feels less threatening to them. Tui settled into our walks reasonably quickly. Sit, down, stay and come, commands the other dogs knew already, took little time for her to master. She just followed what the others did. Thank you, pack! Life was good. Tui was going to be just fine here. Once in a while, I met someone looking for a dog, but when I filled them in on Tui's issue with not bonding, they lost interest. No one wanted a dog that wouldn't bond. If she was adopted locally, would she escape and try to find her way back here? It was a real concern. Was I exaggerating because I didn't want her to leave? I tried to be honest, both with any potential adopter and myself. She had demonstrated that she wasn't going to bond with others, so Tui stayed.

It was about a year and a half later when I received an email from my friend Sarah. She had a friend, Barbara, who had lost her partner and was thinking she might like a dog to help her heal. She had one concern, ok two. Barbara was a cat person, not a dog person. So she had cats and was very concerned about how a dog would interact with her beloved cats. And, she had never had a dog! Sarah called me to talk about the possibility of finding a dog to fit Barbara's requirements and if I had a dog that might work, would I be willing to work with Barbara to make the transition and deal with any issues? I said, "absolutely! " to the second part of that question as that was the easy part! The hard part might be finding a dog that worked. Barbara had described her ideal dog; about three years old, no more than 30 pounds but not a pocket dog. She didn't want a little dog, but it had to be small enough that she could lift it if necessary. She wanted a female, short-haired would be best. And the number one requirement was that this dog likes cats! That often is a tough one, if not impossible.

I told Sara I had a dog that matched that exact description! Tui! I said the only problem was that Tui wasn't good with people. Barbara might like her, but that didn't mean Tui was going to like Barbara. A significant question for me was could I let Tui go? I had accepted that she would stay and she had fit right in so readily. But if it was the right fit, I thought I could adopt her out. This was going to have to be an exceptional home for me to be OK with letting her go. Sarah assured me that Barbara would give her a fantastic home. And, Sarah would be a part of it. I reluctantly agree to a meet and greet.

Barbara and I chatted for some time on the phone about the pros and cons and potential issues with adopting a dog into a cat household. Tui's only real problem was that she wasn't quite house-trained yet. We were working on it, but Tui did still have a few accidents. Barbara's primary concern was that she had never had a dog and that the cats would not accept the dog and vice versa. I reassured her repeatedly that cats were not an issue with Tui. This was a dog that didn't even notice the cat sitting next to her. She just didn't care, didn't react. It was as if the cat wasn't there. I'd never seen a dog so disinterested in cats. I wasn't convinced Barbara believed me. The cats accepting the dog? That might be an issue. My best guess was that since Tui was such a non-reactive dog, the cats would feel safe, and the dog and cats would become good friends in short order.

Barbara and I set a date to meet at the Co-op. I wanted this to happen on neutral ground so that Tui did not feel defensive on her own turf. For me, it would be fascinating to see how she reacted to Barbara. Tui would determine if this was going to be possible at all. Barbara was on the bench at the Co-op when I drove up.

I had Tui in a crate to keep it low key. As I approached the car, she seemed concerned. We'd never done anything like this before. I clipped a leash on her, and we walked over to Barbara sitting on the bench. To my absolute astonishment, Tui walked right up to, and pressed up against, Barbara. She had never done that! She kept her distance from everyone else except me, I was floored! I explained to Barbara that Tui had NEVER done this with another person! And that I took it as a positive sign. Barbara thought she was a really cool dog but had serious concerns about the cat issue and worries that she had never had a dog before. I assured her, yet again, that cats were a non-issue. And, that as dogs go, this was one relaxed dog! Pretty much the ideal first-time dog owner's dog. We sat a little while and talked as she stroked Tui. Tui just sat with her chin on Barbara's knee watching her as we spoke. She asked about food, treats, walks, training, everything she might need to know to make an informed decision. I liked her a lot, and Tui obviously approved. Barbara said she needed to think about it for a few days and she would get back to me. I was good with that. If it didn't happen, Tui had a home with me. I didn't think I would try to find her another home. It was too hard on me. I'd been through that with Sunshine; I wouldn't do it again.

A few days later Barbara called to say she was ready to give it a go. We made arrangements to take Tui to her new home. Barbara just needed a couple of days to get supplies; then we'd make the transfer. Barbara got her a crate. She bought her a new bed. She purchased toys, collar, leash, bowls, the whole 9 yards, everything a dog, or dog owner, would want! I drove Tui down before teaching one morning. Together we explored the yard and house. There was a fenced yard to roam and hang out in when Barbara wasn't home. She even had a dog house! As expected, the cats ran as soon as they saw her; Tui didn't even notice. The cats had plenty of places to hide from the dog if they didn't want to be around her, but I knew it wouldn't take them long to give in to the curiosity. Barbara had a section of the house closed off, so the cats didn't interact with Tui at all. She wanted to keep it slow and give them time to adjust to the idea of a dog in the house. This was all new to them too.

Everything looked great. We agreed to give Tui two weeks to settle in. By then, everything should be fine. It was quiet for a few days, both from Barbara and without Tui. But there were some issues. Barbara called to say that Tui barked at everyone who came to the door. She also had a few accidents in the house. We knew that would be a challenge; I gave Barbara some instructions on how to continue the housetraining. The other issue with Tui was that she was an escape artist! A couple of times, Tui got out, and we had to mount a rescue effort. Tui was gone for a couple of days; Barbara was beside herself with worry. I assured her that this was sometimes part of the process and that I thought Tui would return soon. Thankfully she did. But not before running miles away. Tui didn't come when she was called. At my house, the yard was so small it hadn't been a problem. At Barbara's, she had room to roam. If she wasn't ready to come in, she didn't! Tui also never attempted an escape at my place, so that wasn't something she had learned here. We were going to have to address these issues and fast. As expected, the cats, at least, were no problem. At first, they weren't happy to have a dog in the house, but it didn't take them long to realize that Tui was not a threat. To address the other problems, and just for good dog knowledge, Barbara signed up for training with Julie, a trainer in Santa Fe. Tui learned very fast, and in no time at all, Barbara was feeling confident about owning a dog. That alone would change the dynamic between dog and owner. A dog will pick up on fear and anxiety. Inconsistent training can be disastrous, so I applauded Barbara for all her work with Tui.

Tui came back to stay for a little while when Barbara had to be out of the country. I had offered to take her anytime Barbara needed to board her. Tui knew this as her home, and I loved getting to visit with her. It would be much better than placing her in a kennel, for all of us. I was curious to see how Tui would be when Barbara returned. Tui was so excited to see her she piddled. Tui hadn't done that since I last visited in Santa Fe. She was now Barbara's girl, for sure.

I could not have chosen a better home for this dog! It's even better than having her here because she's an only dog and gets all the attention. She goes for long walks every day, it's just fantastic. I left them to bond and do their work, and after a few months, we would get together so I could see how well Tui was doing; Barbara too! That time came, and we scheduled on a day I was in Santa Fe to teach. I hadn't heard much in a little while, so I was looking forward

Tui 🐾

to seeing where they were in their training and bonding. I arrived in the afternoon. As soon as she saw me, Tui was so excited she piddled. I hugged her and stroked and kissed her. She looked so good! Fit and healthy with all the walks and hikes she and Barbara took together. Barbara had put out some lovely snacks and sat and talked for a little while. She brought me up to date on all they had learned together. I hated to admit it, but I was a bit envious. Barbara was retired and had both the time and the means to do so much with, and for, Tui. Though I was mostly thrilled that the adoption had worked out so well for both of them. When it was time for me to go, I said goodbye to Tui, and she moved close to Barbara with a look on her face that said, "Don't take me away." She was clearly afraid I was there to bring her back home with me. It was so painful to see that look! It was both so beautiful that she was so happy that she wouldn't leave and so gut-wrenching to know I had been replaced! Ultimately that was good too. It was the best for Tui, and it was my work to be able to let go. That would be work I would continue for the rest of my life though. Funny how it can be so good and so hard. I had done my job very well! Clearly, these two were perfect for each other. Still, I cried halfway home. Tears of loss and tears of such complete joy that this had been an ideal adoption. That this neglected, abandoned, sweet, funny dog was able to bond so completely with a new owner despite her dark past was just so beautiful.

Last year, 2018, Barbara had a gathering, the first anniversary of adopting Tui. It was a wonderful dinner with friends. Barbara and I shared the story of Tui, her name, and her adoption. This time I knew Tui would stay by Barbara's side when it was time for me to go. I didn't hurt so much anymore. Instead, I felt happy knowing she and Barbra were meant to be together. Tui was really home.

As I wrapped this story up an email came in celebrating Tui's 5th Birthday! ! What? Five already? Time was flying. Tui's birthday was a total guess and close enough. I forwarded the email to Barbara, with whom I had not had contact since the party for Tui's first adoption anniversary. It was beautiful to connect.

denial
by mariposasun

i don't want to believe it is real
a life taken far too soon

i know i should trust in God when He takes and takes
and takes
but there is a difference between the experiences you
watch from the outside
and when you are living in the wake of a nightmare

now i am one of the billions of members of a club
that i never wanted to be invited to

Dottie

I had intended not to name any favorites, but I have to admit, Dottie's story might be it. Her story was a series of events that went from sad to heart-wrenching, to so totally heartwarming, that the good far outweighed the difficult. The complete turnaround from dark to beautiful makes this story a standout.

I first heard about Dottie through a text message from Megan. Megan was one of the women that helped corral Mitzi into the crate by the side of the road on Highway 75 when she and Tui were dumped. Megan is a rescuer, she's also a breeder. She breeds incredibly beautiful, Olde English bulldogs. And she rescues horses. Megan lives in an area, up in the mountains, where dogs are often dumped. People know that she'll take them in just like we do. Amazing how word gets around! Megan would prefer it not be she who has to deal with the abandoned dogs, but she'd take them in rather than leave them to fend for themselves in the mountains, or worse. One of Megan's dogs had recently whelped a litter, and she had her hands full. She said she could not possibly take Dottie in and hoped I could. Just a few weeks before, I had adopted Tui's puppies out, and I was really in need of a break. But Megan was pretty desperate. She just couldn't handle Dottie and didn't want to take her to the shelter. A pregnant pit mix might be euthanized. It was too risky.

Dottie was a healer/pit mix, white with red markings. She was super sweet and got along well with other dogs. That was a huge plus because I had a house full and couldn't take a dog that wasn't going to get along. I gave in, and Megan drove Dottie down. Megan had named her "Princess." I told Megan I wouldn't call any dog, "Princess!" (I just don't like the name.) "I think I'll call her Dottie!" I said. Megan just laughed, "All my dumped females are called 'Princess.'" Dottie had a perfect egg-shaped spot right on top of her head. "Dottie" was a good name. And yes, she was sweet and gentle and obviously pregnant.

As I do with many of our dogs that come in, the first day they go in the studio kennel with the old dogs who are both dog-friendly. It was late spring, and it was warm, so I didn't have any concerns about a pregnant dog staying out there. I called Taos Vet to get Dottie in for Dr. Jeff to give me an estimate on when she was due. Since she was obviously pregnant, it was probably only a couple of weeks until whelping. They had an opening that afternoon, so we headed for Taos. Dottie rode quietly in the car. I would keep asking myself why anyone would dump this sweet, gentle girl for a long time to come. At the vet, Dottie was calm and cooperative. She seemed a bit scared, but she sat quietly through the entire exam. All 15 minutes worth! Dr. Jeff put the delivery date at two and a half weeks, close enough. We'd be ready. She received her shots without incident, and we headed home. I was glad I had some time before she was due and would be back into puppy care. It is one of the most beautiful experiences I have had, but it is also a tremendous amount of work. For the first two weeks after a litter arrives, mom does all the care and clean up, but once their eyes are open, it changes very quickly! By four weeks old, I am on full-time poop patrol.

After about a week, I started watching for the nesting behavior that indicates that a mother dog is going into labor. I didn't see any signs and didn't expect to see any this early, so I went on about my life. My friend Roy was coming over to help reinforce the fence in the backyard. The dogs had pulled a section down and it was clear we needed a higher fence. We scheduled the work for Wednesday, April 13th. The weather was perfect, and we were both free until the evening when we would head to Peñasco for dinner and an Opera performance.

On that day we also had Mitch, our local handy guy, over to help with pooper scooping and other rescue chores like mending the cattery where the dogs like to jump on it. I went into the studio kennel to check on Dottie before we got fully into the fencing project and noticed that she was showing the first signs of labor. Her water had broken, and she was nesting. "Oh, this is not good!" I thought to myself. She's 10 days early! Could we have been this off on the due date?! I was going with the former as I know from experience how accurate Dr. Jeff is.

I quickly brought her from the studio kennel into the guest bathroom, a.k.a. the whelping room. She climbed into the tub on her own, they all do! I gave her pillows and soft bedding to lie on, and a bowl of water, she'd need it; birthing is hard work! It was 2:00 P.M. I went out and told Roy that she was in labor early and that I was very concerned *AND* that I would not be a lot of help with the fence as I was going to have to watch this whelping closely for signs of distress. I asked Mitch to leave the other duties for now, and help Roy with the fencing. I felt terrible, leaving Roy to work with Mitch, but I was needed elsewhere.

I bounced between bathroom and back yard fencing project not having any way of knowing how soon the first pup would deliver. While I was outside working on the fence for a bit, Dottie gave birth to her first puppy. I returned to the bathroom just as she finished cleaning him up. He was dead, stillborn. I was heartbroken to watch as his lifeless little body flopped around while Dottie frantically licked him trying to stimulate his breathing and heart. It wasn't working so I tried massaging his tiny chest and gently breathing into his little wet nose to try to revive him. I couldn't. I gently laid him down so that Dottie could see that he was gone and be with him for a few minutes to grieve his loss. (And here I am in tears as if I am right back there in the bathroom with Dottie and this beautiful white and grey spotted pit bull mix pup, grieving his loss all over again. So tiny and precious. So devastatingly sad.) As I softly spoke to her, telling her that I was sorry that the puppy was dead, she started to eat the puppy!! At first, I was aghast! How horrible! I gagged as she crunched his body. Why would she do that?! I took the pup away because I just couldn't handle the idea. And, I was so relieved that when she bit him, there was absolutely no response. He truly was gone. Although I do understand they do this in the wild, to not draw predators, we were in my bathroom, so there was no danger. I picked the dead puppy up and held him for her to see and say goodbye. I think she knew he was gone, but I wanted her to understand why I was taking the puppy away. He appeared to be fully formed although Dottie was 10 days early to deliver. Ten days is significant in a dog gestation of about two months. A whole lot of lung and digestive system development happens in those final 10 days; it wasn't looking hopeful.

I had no experience with a premature whelping, but I assumed this was just what happens. The chance of any of the puppies being viable was slim. But I really hoped I was wrong and that she just started with a stillborn. I went back out to help with the fence since there is usually some time between puppies. When I checked again, she had not delivered another puppy yet. I was getting concerned because the interval was quite long. Average is around an hour or less per puppy, she was now going on two hours since the stillborn first pup. I also considered the time might be extended because something was very wrong. Stillbirths took more time as they were harder for the mother dog to deliver. The puppies were small, which was probably helpful in this case. If they took too many hours to whelp, Dottie could be in grave danger. We didn't go to dinner or the Opera performance. I couldn't leave Dottie alone with such a complicated whelping.

I checked on the progress every 15-20 minutes, but the next puppy was slow to whelp. When I went back in at 7:30 if there wasn't a puppy I was going to take Dottie to the emergency vet in Taos, but there was another puppy. This one was alive!! I stroked the pup, a little girl, and helped her latch on to nurse. She seemed to be nursing well, so I left Dottie to nurse and bond. During the evening she gave birth to another stillborn. I stopped checking their genders; I didn't really want to know. I continued to check on Dottie throughout the evening, and by bedtime, it appeared that she was done.

The little female nursed for about an hour or so, but she was weak and couldn't hang on and died. I didn't understand, and Dottie didn't seem to know why this was happening. She looked at me with eyes full of fear and sadness. It was gut-wrenching. I couldn't change it, couldn't make it better or any different, and couldn't make her understand why. I didn't know why! I had the sense from her that this had happened before. When I went to console Dottie she just had a look on her face that said why? Why again? I held the dead puppies out for her to see that they were not alive, but she just didn't seem to understand. It was so difficult and so sad. She was apparently done with labor, no more puppies, none survived. I was exhausted; Dottie was clearly exhausted too, so I went to bed.

When I got up and checked on her in the morning, there were two more puppies she'd given birth to during the night or early morning. One was dead, but one was alive and nursing on his own. He was the largest of the litter and clearly the strongest. Even though he was 10 days premature, he had a powerful suckle. This was so good to see! Through tears of joy and relief, I named him Atlas. It looked like he was going to make it!

I kissed Dottie, and she seemed so happy and proud. To be sure he was getting enough nutrition, I did supplemental feedings between nursings. This also gave me the chance to get a good look at him and bond. He was a dark brown, sable coated boy. Though he was the largest he was still quite small, especially given Dottie's size - she was about 60 pounds. This little guy was only about 8 oz.; he should have been double that size or more. I was sure she was done now, so I left her to care for the one surviving boy. When I checked in an hour or so later, there was another live pup!!! This one was a little white and black spotted girl. Like her sister that had lived for a short time, she was tiny. But she, like Atlas, nursed well. I pleaded to the universe: "Oh please, oh please let them make it!" With this sixth pup, I was absolutely sure she was done whelping, but I would watch her closely for any signs of a retained puppy or placenta. If she died, the puppies had no chance. I'm not sure I had the strength to handle losing her. Losing the pups was hard enough!

Dottie wouldn't leave the puppies. She wouldn't even go out to potty. She would hold it till she literally exploded in the bathroom. I would return to find copious amounts of urine and feces. In almost unreal volumes. She would hold her poo for days rather than go out! I just couldn't get upset over that, and, I didn't blame her. She was so afraid that if she left, even for a minute, that they would die. Anytime I have a whelping or queening in the bathroom I'm well prepared! The entire floor is covered in plastic and puppy pads. It's still a chore, but it helps contain any mess. Thankfully, after a few days of this, she would venture outside to potty. That certainly made things easier for me, and for Dottie's bladder.

After a few days, we lost the little girl. On one of my check-ins, I saw that she wasn't nursing or moving. I tried to revive her, but it was of no use. Again, just not strong enough to survive. Atlas continued to nurse well, and it was clear he was growing! Dottie was a great mom; I was so excited that she'd have one surviving baby to love.

My excitement sadly would be short-lived. After about five days, he started to lose weight. I rushed him into the vet where I was told, "He's nursing well so he'll be fine." But he wasn't "fine." He was failing. I could just feel it! It is simply called failure to thrive. When puppies are this premature, their digestive systems haven't developed enough to absorb the nutrients in the mother's milk. So, even though he was eating well and getting supplemental feedings, his body couldn't assimilate enough of the nutrients to keep him alive.

Atlas was exactly one week old, I was sitting by the tub, stroking him as he nursed. Stroking always made him suckle with more enthusiasm. I had my hand on his back as he nursed when suddenly his entire body went absolutely stiff and he died instantly. One massive, shuddering, seizure and that was it. He didn't suffer, but Dottie did. She cried out as if to ask once again, "Why?!" She went into a deep depression. Dogs have depression just like people do, and it was hard to witness. She wouldn't eat or go out. She just wanted to lie in the tub where she could smell the scent of her now deceased puppies.

I had the puppies in the freezer until they could be buried or cremated and I would take them out for Dottie to see, hoping she would understand they were gone, it didn't seem to help. She just gave me that imploring look. Why?! She looked so sad. I was deeply concerned for her life. Would she stop eating? Would she lose her will to live? Especially if this was not the first litter to die, would she make it? I didn't want to lose her too! She was the sweetest girl and would be a great addition to someone's family once she was spayed and healed. What could I do to help this poor momma? I grabbed the phone and called our local shelters, and all of the vets we work with, to let them know that I had a nursing mom in case any abandoned litters or puppies needed to be removed from an aggressive mother. I had a wonderful surrogate. Dottie was absolutely full of milk, and she was prepared to nurse six good-sized puppies. No one needed a surrogate mom, and it killed me, I was sure this would be so good for Dottie, but it wasn't to be. A couple of times, I got the brush off. But I reminded them of how quickly things can change! A call could come in at any time that a mother dog was hit and killed or left her pups, or wasn't producing enough milk for a large litter, etc.. There are many reasons why a surrogate might be needed.

A dog can nurse other species in a pinch; someone had to need this sweet mom and her full teats. No one did. Then, about a week later, I got a call from the puppy coordinator at Stray Hearts in Taos. She asked if I thought Dottie would surrogate a litter that was abandoned at the Taos Pueblo. I said I bet she would!! I canceled all my appointments that day threw on some clothes and headed to Taos. Since Dottie hadn't nursed a for the week, it would take about 24 hours for her to come fully back into milk. But we had to try!

We arrived at the shelter about 45 minutes later and were taken back into an isolation room. This room was a sterile exam room where they bring dogs that are ill, for diagnosis. It had just been cleaned so safe for puppies to be on the floor. The room was all a light grey-blue, very sterile looking. There was a heavy door that leads to the isolation area in the middle of the south wall, between two counters. This is where I would sit. Often, at the house, I would sit in the tub with Dottie in my lap while she nursed Atlas. There was a second heavy door with a safety glass window that looked out into a hallway. I sat facing it.

I suggested we do the same thing here, so we spread a blanket. I sat down on the floor and straddled Dottie. She then pressed up against me, wondering why she was here, I'm sure. The staff brought in the first puppy and set it down in front of Dottie. There were a half dozen people in the room to watch how this went. The room was it was silent. Dottie sniffed the puppy and then shifted her body to expose her belly. The puppy waddled over and started nursing immediately. So far so good, but you could've cut the tension in that room with a knife. I was probably the only one that was absolutely sure Dottie would take to these puppies like they were her own. But the shelter staff didn't know; I did. Sometimes with a surrogate, she will refuse to nurse the puppies, or she will become extremely aggressive and try to hurt or kill puppies that aren't her own. I knew this would not be the case with Dottie. Since the first puppy was accepted and nursing so well, we brought in puppy number two. Everyone stopped breathing. The anticipation was palpable.

I tried to reassure everyone, but they would have to see it for themselves. Just like the first, Dottie sniffed this puppy, then she lay down to expose her belly and the puppy hungrily latched on! We repeated this with number three with the same result. "Just bring them all in!" I cried with tears running down my face. By now, word had gotten around the shelter, and everyone had to come to have a peak in to witness this remarkably beautiful event. Everyone was in tears as soon as they looked in. Dottie had now laid completely out with her head on my right thigh, and she looked at me with a look that said, "where have you been hiding my puppies?! " I had no way to explain that hers had died and these were new puppies, but in time it wouldn't matter anyway.

We added puppies four, five, and six together as it was so apparent that Dottie was not just going to accept them, but adopt them as her own! Tears were flowing, and shutters were clicking as we captured this incredible moment. It was precisely what Dottie needed. And these puppies would not have survived without her. It turns out that this litter was precisely the same age and the same number as her own litter. They were of different breed mixes though. The mom of these puppies was a Chow mix, and by looking at the puppies, there were at least three dads of very different breeds. The puppies were quite fat and healthy. This was good because it would take a little time for Dottie to come back into full milk.

Dottie and I loaded up the truck, with the puppies in a large crate, and headed home. I'm not sure who was happier - me or Dottie! What had been a devastating loss was now a beautiful rescue, and one that didn't often happen. That was because this litter of puppies came from the Taos Pueblo. The Pueblo is sovereign, and they don't like any intrusion. They often have a dog overpopulation problem but will not accept assistance outside their own people. They do things their way, and we respect that. In this case, a woman on the Reservation witnessed the mother dog abandon the puppies. She scooped them up and put them in a crate and took them to the shelter where she knew they'd have the best chance of survival. We were so grateful to her. I can tell you Dottie was too!

I put Dottie and company in the bathroom as the puppies were still only a couple of weeks old. Though there wasn't much room in the tub, I climbed in to stroke her while she nursed. I wanted to be there every minute! At first, Dottie would look at me with that look she gave me at the shelter. She was sure they were her pups! Then the look softened to a look that said, "Thank you for my puppies." I could only tell her, "You are welcome." Before too long, she didn't give me those looks anymore. We all just settled into what would have been the norm if her pups had survived. I only needed to supplement feeding for a few days, and she was back in full milk.

Looking at the litter, some were part shepherd, a few part lab, and one that didn't fit in at all! Five of the six had short coats like a lab. Two were solid black. One black with a white chest, possible a heeler mix. Two were tan with black like a shepherd. Most had just a stub of a tail. One had no tail at all. It is possible they were born that way, but we'd never know. Then there was the black and white curly haired male. He was a third the size of the other puppies, who were all fat and larger breed mixes. This little guy looked to be half miniature poodle! Nothing like the others. Since a litter can have as many dads as there are puppies we do sometimes see litters like this. All that really mattered was that they were adorable, healthy, and going to be just fine!

For the next two months, we did the usual; for the first two weeks, the bathroom was home. I would go in and just sit and marvel at it all. Dottie would smother me with kisses of gratitude and love. I handled the puppies every day to socialize them so that when they were ready for adoption, they would be accustomed to people and willing to bond with a new owner. Puppy breath is intoxicating, so they had plenty of attention, and I received a healthy dose of puppy love. At four weeks, when they became much more active, we started taking time outside in the small dog yard. The little dogs were crated so that Dottie and puppies could be out without the other dogs in the way. Dottie sat watch over them and nursed and cleaned them as needed. Just watching her mothering this clan made my heart sing! I took more photos of this litter than of any other before, or since. It will stand out as one of the hardest and most beautiful rescues I have had the honor to be part of.

The puppies all grew and progressed as they should. As they got bigger, their breeds were becoming more evident. The tan male with no tail may have been part corgi. He was a short fellow, low to the ground, and is the puppy on the cover of this book. Puppies and surrogate mother thrived. If I was home, they were outside. If I was out, they had the safety of the bathroom. Having them out daily made the indoor clean up a bit less taxing. Six large breed puppies get to be a whole lot of work! Dottie agreed. At about six weeks, the mother dog will start to wean the puppies. After a few minutes of nursing, Dottie would stand up and leave the tub. Previously she would nurse until all the puppies had full bellies and fell asleep. It was time to start weaning. I added a baby gate to the bathroom door, so Dottie could jump it and have time away from the pups when she needed to. This also allowed her time to be part of the inside dog family. She was sweet and got along well with all of the other dogs. She was such a love! But she would soon need a home of her own.

The puppies stayed with me for nine weeks until they were weaned and we arranged for them to transfer to Colorado. We have a couple of people who drive transfer from our area to three or four different rescue organizations in Colorado about once a week. I met our transfer driver in Taos early one morning. All puppies had had their first shots, worming, and kennel cough vaccines, so they were ready to roll. Each is given a number and placed in a travel crate. Litters usually travel together to provide them with the comfort of litter mates. I kissed each plump puppy one last time as they were loaded into the Jeep.

By nine weeks, I'm ready to see them go, but it is still so hard to say goodbye. This litter would go to Colorado Puppy Rescue. I like CPR because they post photos of each puppy on adoption day and, later, a picture of the puppy with their new family. Just days after the puppies arrived in Colorado they were put up for adoption; all six were adopted out in one day! That wasn't really surprising as they were well socialized, sweet little fur balls.

So, now what to do with Dottie? Once the puppies were transferred, Dottie went to the vet to finish her shots and to be spayed, so she was ready for adoption herself. She was young, maybe two to two and a half years old. She was great with other dogs, good with cats, good with people. Why she was dumped? I can't wrap my head around that. All I can think was that she was pregnant, again, and the owner just didn't want to deal with that. She wasn't a dog that needed to stay with me because she was so well-adjusted and I didn't need her to stay with me. I had too many! As much as I adored her, I knew I could find her a fabulous home.

I posted Dottie to our local email service called the Town Crier, on our DAPS' Facebook page, and on my personal Facebook page. It wasn't long before the phone rang. Remember that couple I told you about in Peñasco who own the restaurant and found Turnip? Their old alpha female Delilah, the one who was not friendly to Turnip, developed aggressive bone cancer, and had passed away a couple of weeks prior. Kai had decided to retire, so she was home most of the day. It was the right timing to bring in a new dog. Dottie was so mellow, sweet, and gentle, I thought this was an absolutely perfect match! We arranged a meeting, and I brought Dottie up to their house so they could meet her and see how she did with the cats. No reaction, no problems. I figured given a little time Dottie and the cats would be curled up together on the sofa. After our initial visit, I asked both Ki and Kai what they thought. Kai thought she was perfect, as did I. But Ki wasn't sure, she needed to think about it. She wasn't sure she was ready for another dog just yet. I told her I totally understood. After the loss of a beloved pet, everyone is different. Some, like me, adopt again right away. Not that a new dog can replace the old one, but I find some puppy love is a powerful healer! Others need to wait. Sometimes weeks or months, sometimes years. Everyone grieves differently, and I never force a decision on adoption. I told Ki and Kai that Dotty would be with me for a while and that I didn't have anyone else looking to adopt her, so they had some time to think it over. Two days later, I got the call, "we want to adopt her!" I wasn't the least bit surprised, but I was ecstatic! I couldn't think of a more perfect home. Kai asked if they could rename her, I said of course. For a short time, she was Ramona, I believe, but that didn't fit, so she ended up being named Sadie. I've always loved the name, Sadie! Though she'll always be Dottie to me. This is, so far, my favorite rescue story. It started out so tragically and ended so perfectly.

And it got even better! Paula, Megan's friend who had helped crate Mitzi, needed to find a new home for one of her dogs. Her rheumatoid arthritis was getting worse and she couldn't manage so many dogs. Her little Chihuahua mix, Thunder, was available for adoption. It was very hard for her to give the dog up and she pleaded with me to be sure that Thunder would only go to a good home. I promised, as I knew how terribly difficult this was. I posted Thunder to the Town Crier and guess who had been looking for a small dog to add to the family?! We did a dog introduction that went off without a hitch so now Sadie had a little friend. Paula knew Ki and Kai and could visit Thunder, now Lulu.

Prayer of a Stray
author unknown

Dear God, Please send me somebody who'll care!
I'm tired of running, I'm sick with despair.
My body is aching, it's so racked with pain,
And Dear God, I pray as I run in the rain,
That someone will love me and give me a home.
A warm cozy bed and a big juicy bone . . .

Photo by Judy Pearson

Blondie

A few years ago Christine, who worked in Española on occasion, called to ask if she could bring two puppies over. There was a house where an unspayed female had puppies once or twice a year. In 2012 Christine, my husband and I went down to the trailer where the puppies lived and pulled two out from under it. The single wide was not occupied as it had recently caught fire. It provided excellent protection for the pups. We had to crawl under it to retrieve two adorable shepherd mixes that we named Trailer and McCurdy. They went off to Colorado after a visit to the Veterinarian. The puppies that Christine was now calling about were from the same mother, shepherd mixes, but this time two girls. I told Christine to bring them over as the foster kennel was available. She named the blond puppy "Blondie" after the musician, but couldn't think of a name for the black and tan. When they arrived, it was instantly clear that Blondie was the boss. She was a bit fear aggressive and didn't appreciate my attempts to put a collar on her. Her sister was shy but very sweet and allowed a collar without issue. I named her "Toots." Like Tootsie, since she was so sweet, and it fit well with

"Blondie." I immediately arranged for a transfer to Colorado as these were older puppies and soon would be too old to send north. A transfer was scheduled for the next Wednesday morning. I drove them to Taos then turned around and headed to Santa Fe to teach. I was teaching on Wednesdays back then. When I dropped them off, Toots went quickly into the transfer crate. Blondie did not. I had to pick her up and put her in with Toots. She fought me, but I eventually succeeded. I drove away with an uneasy feeling about Blondie.

Later that afternoon, I received a call that Blondie had been rejected by the rescue because of her fear aggression. I had spent as much time as I could while she was here to help her get over it, but it may not have been enough time. The other issue I had with Blondie was that she could get out of any enclosure! The two girls were in a 10x10x6' chain link kennel, and Blondie was always running loose! They had a dog house for comfort, and I watched as Blondie jumped up on the house then over the fence with ease. I moved the dog house to the center of the kennel so she couldn't use it to jump out; she dug under. She was proving to be a handful. In the short time we had together, she calmed down considerably. She was happy to come over for treats and belly rubs, I could adjust her collar without issue, and she was learning basic commands very quickly. With a little more training, she would become a fabulous dog. But she wasn't there yet. The transfer driver called to tell me I had to pick her up. I called around for a volunteer to meet her in Questa or Angel Fire, but I could not find anyone available. Blondie needed to be spayed so I suggested she be dropped at the Taos Vet and I'd pick her up after surgery the next day. Thankfully the vet could take her and hold her overnight. The transfer driver was not pleased that she had to go back through Taos, but it was the best solution I could offer.

When I arrived the next morning, I was greeted by the Veterinarian with, "You're here for that crazy dog." I chuckled and said I was but insisted that she wasn't crazy, she was fear aggressive and just needed some time and training. He suggested I consider euthanasia as he didn't think she was stable. I said, "No." I shook his head but lead me to the recovery room to get her. Blondie and I piled into the car and went home.

I tried kenneling her again, but it quickly became clear she was never going to stay in an enclosure, so I gave it up. She decided she was home. She remained in the yard as my protector, though she wasn't aggressive at all, but she was imposing. My property is nearly an acre and a half. Adjacent is an empty lot of similar size that friends purchased as an investment. Blondie could run free across the three acres. Over the next couple of years, she became a much-loved member of the neighborhood. Buddy, another free-roaming non-aggressive neighborhood dog, became her best friend. He would spend every afternoon playing and napping out in the yard. At night Blondie slept in her crate in my studio to avoid barking or altercations with coyotes, bears, or mountain lions. She had indeed become the fabulous dog I thought she would. It just took a little time, love, and patience. Life with and for Blondie was good.

I teach figure skating on Sundays in Santa Fe at the beautiful Genoveva Chavez Community Center. The man in my life lived in Santa Fe, so I spent my weekends with him and returned on Monday morning. When I woke that Monday, I told Mark that I felt awful. I was in a very dark place mentally, but had no recollection of a bad dream (or nightmare) nor was I sick. We had had a very full weekend, so I thought my Chronic Fatigue had caught up with me. I have days when I have pushed too hard and just can't function. But this felt different. I wasn't depressed, but I couldn't really explain how I felt. Mark asked if I was coming down with something. I said, "No, I don't think so." Though there was an odd feeling in the pit of my stomach.

Mark made coffee and brought it to me in bed. He made excellent coffee, and it did seem to help. It got me up, so I went down to the kitchen and finished making the breakfast he had started; our go-to, oatmeal. The weather was turning cold, so some sweet hot-cereal sounded great. He started cooking, and I'd finish it up with fruit and nuts, cinnamon and maple syrup. He sat me on his lap and held me. Coffee and breakfast helped, but I couldn't shake the looming darkness. We finished breakfast. Mark went to work, and I headed back home.

The drive home from Santa Fe that morning was uneventful. I felt a little less of the weight of the gloom, but my gut was still unsettled. When I pulled up to my gate, I expected Blondie to greet me as I unlocked it. She didn't. That wasn't all that unusual. Sometimes she'd wander off to visit the neighbors' dogs but if she did she'd soon come trotting up when she heard my approach. More often than not with Buddy close behind. From the gate, I enter directly in front of the house. Just to the left of the drive is my studio. The storage room, closest to the road, has a kennel off the back. I can't see it as it is blocked by my kiln barn. It used to be my mini horse barn, a three stall wood and steel custom barn sized for my miniature horses. Since I had to rehome the horses when I divorced, I now used the barn as a kiln and storage barn. I could hear the kennel dogs barking their greeting, but still no Blondie. As I pulled past the studio, I could see the metal storage shed over by the fence, halfway between the studio and the house. My neighbors' dogs Zia and Trixie were in front of the shed. Trixie was lying down, and Zia was standing at her feet. My thought was that Jeannie had left Blondie in the studio. That would be good. I looked back at Trixie and Zia as I got out of my car and thought it odd that Zia was drooling profusely. My gaze moved to Trixie, and it was then that I saw the blood. Trixie was covered in blood, and she was panting heavily. Like she had been running or fighting! I told them both to go home and screamed, "Where is Blondie?! " Zia left quickly; Trixie got slowly up and limped away. It was then that I knew they had been fighting. I called for Blondie, but she didn't come. My heart was racing as I feared the worst. I ran to the back fence to see if Blondie was there, I had had a dog fight there before, but no, no Blondie. As I ran back to where the dogs had been, I saw blood on the front of the shed. I dropped to my knees to look underneath the shed; I just started howling! There was Blondie under the shed, not moving. I was sure she was dead; then saw her side rise and fall with her breath. I grabbed a heavy blanket and ran into the house. My gut was in knots. I grabbed the truck keys hanging on a nail on the side of the cabinet above my dryer. I turned and flew into the bathroom and my system emptied.

I knew I had little time. I slid under the shed on my belly and grabbed Blondie by the hind feet. It was the only way I was going to get her out. I barely fit in the space. It is a metal shed set up on 2x4s to level it and keep it off the ground. The dogs loved to hang out under the building in the hot weather. It was cool and gave them shade, but for me, it was a tight fit; as I moved farther under it became even more uncomfortable. Blondie had crawled as far back as she could to protect herself from further attack. As I dragged my beloved dog into the morning sunlight, I saw the extent of the injury to her right hind leg.

A large chunk of her leg was gone. There was a gaping hole where her hamstring muscle used to be! "Noooo!!" All I could do was scream "Noooo!" Over and over. My beautiful girl was dying, and there was *nothing* I could do!! Why did the dogs attack when they had been running around together for months without incident? I got her out in what seemed like a split second, picked up her limp body and placed her in the back of the rescue truck on the thick, soft blanket. I begged her to hold on. When I pulled my hands out from under her, I realized I was covered in blood. Both palms and my entire right arm were soaked. I had only seen the noticeable bites; clearly, there were more. She was unresponsive though we did make eye contact. "I'm so sorry," croaked from my now raw throat. I wondered if she was paralyzed. Was her neck broken? I couldn't tell but, pulling her out with the massive bite on her leg should have caused her pain and she should have reacted with a yelp or whimper or growl, but she made no noise; nothing.

Absolutely no reaction, and I knew that was a bad sign, really bad. Blondie was in deep shock, and time was short. I left without closing my gate and headed to Española to the closest Vet Clinic, Cottonwood. They have been one of our go-to's for decades. Doc Ramsay is one of the best vets anywhere; certainly in New Mexico. Doc has worked miracles for us and many others. But it was Monday and knowing Mondays were crazy; they probably couldn't even get her in, but hoping with the extent of her injuries, that they would find a way to help her. I really thought euthanasia was the only option at this point. I did not want her to suffer any longer, and I didn't know how long she had been under the shed alone, in pain, bleeding to death.

And why is it that in a dire emergency the guy in front of you, on a rural road with no room to pass, won't even drive the speed limit!? I rode his bumper hoping he'd pull over and let me by. He didn't. I was sending telepathic messages to make him understand this was an emergency! He wasn't receptive. Blondie only had minutes to live. I needed to move! Once we hit the main road, I passed illegally, making sure it was clear before I did. On the way down, I kept calling the vet clinic but only heard a busy signal time and time again. I thought, "screw it," we'd figure it out later! I had hoped to give the clinic a heads up but just couldn't get through! I kept an eye on Blondie in the rearview mirror. I could see that she was still breathing and once to my shock and awe, she tried to sit up! She wasn't paralyzed, but she could not lift her head. It hung heavily as she tried to look at me. I told her to lie down and rest, we'd be there soon. When we arrived, I was struck by the lack of cars in the parking lot. It was Monday, it should have been full. Maybe this was our lucky day? I burst in, and the waiting room was empty, very strange. The only one in the room was a Vet Tech I knew. I said I had an emergency, that Blondie had been attacked by loose dogs. The tech came out, took one look at Blondie, and ran back in for a gurney. We had her out of the truck in no time! We took her back to the surgery area and laid her on the floor. All of the tables were in use. Dr. Olivas came back to assess the wounds. I told her I thought we needed to put her down. She listened to Blondie's heart and respiration, took her temp, which was high at 104, indicating infection. To my surprise, she suggested we try to save her. Dr. O

Blondie 🐾

gave Blondie an injection so she wouldn't be in pain and put her on IV fluids. Her gum color was terrible, ashen, she was in shock, and she had lost a lot of blood, but we had to try. Her color started to improve, but she had a long way to go. If she stabilized, we could get her into surgery to clean out the massive leg and neck wounds. She'd need numerous surgeries, but she could heal. As we waited, I put a call into Animal Control. Our AC Officer said he'd stop in and take my statement. He arrived as promised and came back to see how bad it was. I stood up to greet him, and he looked at the blood now covering most of my upper body.

I looked down at my hands, stunned by the sheer volume of blood. My dog's life was literally on my hands and I could do nothing more to save her. The Officer didn't shake my hand. I gave him all the details. He asked if I'd taken a photo of the two dogs in my yard. Incredulously I said, "No. I was too busy trying to save my dog! " I was told there was nothing AC could do, but I could take the owners to court for the vet fees. I really wasn't up for a court battle. I told him the owners of the dogs that attacked were co-operating thus far. He thought that was good and left. I went back to holding Blondie, letting her know I loved her and that if she needed to go, it was OK.

Her breathing suddenly changed, becoming raspy and labored. Dr. O stopped back in to see how she was doing, "I think she is checking out. Her breathing just changed; it doesn't sound good." I told her. She then felt her chest and listened with a stethoscope. "You're right. She is checking out. She is going into respiratory failure. Do you want me to help her go? Or do you just want her to go naturally," I said, "As long as she isn't in any pain I'll let her go naturally." I held her in my lap and talked to her until she took her last breath. I was glad she was no longer suffering, but I was so angry that she died like this! She was just three years old! (It has been a year and a half since that awful day and I am editing through tears. The images of that day are as vivid as they were then. Though sadly, other memories are fading.) This was so unfair to her and so awful for me.

Back home, I spoke with both owners of the dogs who mauled her. One felt horrible and offered to pay the full bill. She also promised to contain her dog so she could never do it again. The other owner said, "Prove it!" I couldn't prove it. No one had seen the fight. Bob, next door, had heard it but thought it was the usual morning fence fight. I knew both dogs; both had been visiting for months. They had had bark fights but never anything more. Blondie and Turnip loved to fence fight each morning for a couple of minutes, then they would go about their day quietly. The mauling occurred at the time that the fence fighting generally took place. I suspected that my dogs were engaged in their morning ritual when the other two arrived, and it escalated to a deadly fight. Had it only been one of the two dogs, there most likely would not have been a fatal brawl, but these two dogs together had bad chemistry. There have been no issues since. Trixie has shown up in my yard, but she has never done anything beyond some fence barking. She goes home as soon as I tell her to leave. Zia and her owner moved away. They do visit once in a while and when they do Zia is in the yard. She also has not caused any trouble. Out here, I have the right to shoot her if she is on my land, but I cannot, and will not, do that. It would not bring Blondie back, would not avenge her death, it would only cause needless suffering for someone else. I could not harm an animal for an owner's negligence.

Blondie died two days ago. Coming home is so hard; my yard feels so empty without her. The soul-searing pain of her death is momentarily eclipsed by the complete disbelief that she is gone. I have lost many dogs over the years. Those were easy compared to this.

Mark Twain

"If you pick up a starving dog
and make him prosperous he will not bite you.
This is the principal difference
between a dog and man."

Alcalde Dog

I was in Santa Fe, which is an hour south of Dixon. I teach Figure Skating at the rink there twice a week. My cell phone rang. Barked, actually, as my ringtone is barking dogs. It always gets attention and smiles from unsuspecting people close by. Since it was Hallie calling I took the call. She was distraught. There was a dog in Alcalde, a community halfway between Santa Fe and Dixon, that was tied to a tree. It was in front of a house in the hot sun, without water, shade, or shelter. The tree was small with few branches so afforded very little shade, if any. She wasn't free to go get the dog, so she was calling to ask me to go down.

I had actually just finished teaching, so I could head that way, but it would be an hour before I could get there. I suggested that she have Kim call Jennifer, who is on our board, to see if she could take Kim down. Kim doesn't drive, but she is a top-notch rescuer. Jennifer called to say they had it covered and someone would get back to me and let me know if the dog was OK. Hallie was concerned that it was dead as it didn't move when she drove by earlier. I was just leaving the rink when Jeannie called to tell me not to hurry. My heart sank. I was sure they had gotten there too late, and the dog died of heatstroke. That is an awful way to die.

Jeannie was laughing!! "What?" I asked. I think it took three attempts for Jeannie to tell me, "It was a fake dog!" She was laughing so hard I couldn't understand what she was saying! "A fake dog? What are you talking about?!" I implored. It made no sense! "Do you mean it is plastic? A plastic dog??" I asked. That, of course, sent her into another fit of laughter. After a minute - or five, she said, "No, not plastic. (Pause for laughter.) "You know (laughter) those steel (more laughter) imports?" She need say no more! I couldn't stop laughing. I told Jeannie I had to talk to Jennifer! I called and Jennifer, Kim and Leela, Jennifer's teen aged daughter, were still in the car. Jennifer put me on speaker, and as soon as I said I'd just talked to Jeannie who was quite literally dying of laughter they lost it. All three were in hysterics in Jennifer's car and me in mine! Oh, how I wish I could have been there!

Kim begged me not to share this with anyone. Hallie thought it was humiliating. "You have to be kidding! This is one for the record!" I replied. "Just too funny NOT to share!" I said through my giggles. I told them I was going to go find this "dog" for myself! I had to see it! Jennifer described where it was; I knew the house. I headed out, still laughing. When I arrived in Alcalde, I had to circle the block twice to find the "dog." Hallie was blind in one eye and had found it easily! Why couldn't I? That thought just started the giggles all over again. I was just coming out to the highway on round two when I saw it! There it stood under a small tree which threw very little shade. But it wasn't even a dog! It was a rusty sheet metal *coyote*. A metal yard sculpture. The kind you find at the Import store! I remembered seeing it months ago, but, of course, paid no attention to it! We miss Hallie, but she sure left us laughing.

LONESOME
by Donna Lou McPherren

Little Puppy, sitting there
In the field mid daisies fair
wary eyed you look at me.
Are you lost? Or could it be
someone put you in this place
all alone this to face.
Soon the sun will fade from sight
and the day will turn to night.
You have no drink or food to eat.
Come---I will take you home with me.
Little things need loving care.
Perhaps that is why
God put me here.

Josie

In the summer of 2016, I heard from numerous people about a dog that had likely been dumped. He was seen running along the highway in Dixon between the Post Office and the Community Center. I was asked if I knew anything about this dog. I didn't until Nan and Steve called to tell me about him. They had seen this dog running along the highway for a couple of months, and Steve had started to socialize him. It was Steve who named him Joey. Nan and Steve had recently lost their old dog and adopted a young dog, a pointer mix, called Shanti. Joey adored Shanti. Their relationship was going to help make it much easier for Steve to socialize Joey as the two dogs played together beautifully. It was summer, it was warm, so they left the front door open often to catch any breeze and cool the house. One day Joey just invited himself in! Steve and Nan soon discovered it wasn't just to play with Shanti. Joey loved to steal her toys. Joey loved dog toys!

I am so grateful when other dog people take it upon themselves to take on a dog like Joey. Nan and Steve could handle it all by themselves. They would periodically check in with me and ask for advice or guidance but didn't expect me to do the work. I was all for it. I'd heard from others, like Tommy, that Joey hung out at their houses too. A couple of people on his route had been feeding Joey and attempting to get close, but Nan and Steve were the most successful at this point. So, like Albert, Joey had a daily route. Jeannie asked me if I knew anything about the dog that Tommy had told her about when she ran into him at the Co-op. It does sometimes amaze me how word of dumped or stray dogs gets around so quickly here. I told Jeannie about Nan and Steve working on socializing him with the hope that once he was socialized perhaps, we could help adopt him out. I don't think Nan and Steve wanted to keep him though they would consider it. They were quite dog-savvy. They had rescued a few in their time, and I was confident in their ability to handle Joey.

Steve called periodically to give me updates on how he was doing with Joey. Things like, "He let me rub his belly!" Steve would be so excited as he relayed the news. A couple of weeks after talking to Steve about how Joey liked Shanti's toys, I received the fateful phone call. Joey, while playing with Shanti, ran into the road and bit a pedestrian. Michele is a local, known by almost everyone, who walks down the road on her daily constitutional. On her daily walks Michele is often harassed by loose dogs but rarely has one actually bitten. We don't know why Joey ran out and bit her totally unprovoked, but he did. I called Michele to be sure she was getting the necessary medical attention; she was. I also wanted to allow her to tell her version of the event; she did. It was pretty much as Steve had described. Joey and Shanti had been playing in the house with the front door open as usual. Joey dropped the toy he had just stolen from Shanti and bolted up to the road and bit Michele. The bite was a puncture and a laceration. Not awful but bad enough to cause concern and pain. Joey had come close to biting the Achilles tendon which would have been a much worse bite. I told both Steve and Michele what was required in this situation, and they both understood. Our County ordinance requires that any dog that bites and doesn't have proof of rabies vaccination be in a 10-day quarantine at the pound. In our case, that is the Española Valley

Humane Society. But now we had a serious problem. No one knew where Joey was. I called Tommy to see if he had seen Joey. Tommy said, "Ha! He's here in my yard now." I immediately called Steve to have him meet me at Tommy's with some treats to see if we could try to at least get a slip leash around the dog and take him in for quarantine. I was also very concerned that if he stayed loose, he would bite again. We would much rather handle a situation like this ourselves, if possible than have to call in Animal Control. Sometimes that's a really big "IF," and I was getting the sense that this one may be huge. As I waited for Steve, I became acquainted with the dog at Tommy's. He was pretty shy but seemed very sweet. He was reluctant to come up for treats, but I thought over time, I could gain his trust. If not, we would trap him. As I was assessing the dog's behavior, I concluded that he was a husky/heeler mix. A gorgeous medium-sized, red and white dog. We use the term "red" for several different colors in the red family, like orange. This dog was red/orange and white. He had the prick ears like both breeds and was thickly coated like a husky. His body shape was somewhere between a husky and heeler. It was more square like a heeler with the shorter legs as well. His muzzle too was a cross between the two breeds. Not as blunt as a husky but not quite as pointed as a Heeler. The coat was thick like a husky, but he had foreleg speckles like a heeler. And the glorious husky tail; well furred, thick and fluffy, curling back around to the base. A gorgeous dog. When I got closer, I realized he wasn't a he. He was a she! While I was mulling the gender issue, Steve arrived with a container of tripe. What dog would turn that down? (Personally, I thought it was absolutely disgusting! But I'm not a dog.) Steve squatted down and held his hand out for "Joey" to come over and take a treat. He was very aloof. Steve turned to me and said, "He's acting like he doesn't know me." "You keep calling him he but he's not a he, he is a she." I returned, more confused than before. How could he have made that mistake when it was so obvious? "No." Steve said, "I've seen his equipment, and he is definitely male! " I gave him a look and nodded at the dog. At that point, Steve's head snapped around, and we both looked at the dog. He said, "This isn't the same dog! " Now it was starting to make sense! "Joey has a more rounded face, and he doesn't have the white blaze on his forehead." It was at that moment we realized we had two dogs running loose! A brother and sister probably dumped about two months ago at 8 eight to 10 weeks old. I had a pretty good idea about whose puppies they were. I did suspect the father, the husky, belonged to a friend of mine. He had promised to get his dog neutered, but I later found out he had not! (I ran into the owner and told him about the pups. He said he wanted to see them. Joey had gone to quarantine, but I had photos of the female. When he saw them, he said: "Yup, she has his face!" I think he was kind of proud that his dog was the daddy. He asked if he was in trouble. I said no, but this is why I asked you to neuter your dog. Even if the father dog was neutered, he could still be potent for a few weeks after neutering, so litters happen.) The dog who lived next door to the husky daddy was a red heeler and her owners do not spay or neuter their dogs. They aren't happy that the dog gets pregnant, but they don't seem to make the connection. Sigh! This is something we deal with regularly. So the neighbor dogs mated, and when they couldn't find homes for all the puppies, they dumped them on the highway in town. We can't prove it, so we have no recourse. We have a good no-kill shelter, but people know if they dump them DAPS will find a way to help the dogs.

It quickly became apparent that we were not going to be able to catch Joey easily. We had to call Animal Control to come and grab him. They needed to get a full report from Michelle about the bite incident as well. Nan and Steve were fantastic in handling this whole issue. They worked with our local Animal Control Officer and caught Joey with relative ease. I wasn't there to witness the capture, but I suspect he went back to Nan and Steve's so they would not have had to chase him down. Joey was then taken to the Shelter for a 10-day quarantine hold. It takes 10 days for rabies to present when a dog is infected. If the dog shows signs of disease, they are euthanized, and their brain is sent in for testing. If they test positive, the bite victim must start rabies vaccine shots immediately. Once a human shows symptoms, there is no cure, so the timing is critical. We don't see rabies in domestic dogs here. Once in a while an infected bat, skunk or raccoon is found, but almost never in dogs or cats. So we really weren't concerned that Joey was infected. He was negative.

I have held dogs on quarantine hold here in my kennels, but I didn't have any room with Tui and her pups not yet adopted out, so Joey had to go to the Shelter. Once they had him in their system, the Shelter called me to ask if anyone would be picking Joey up at the end of his quarantine. I said no. I had no one that would take him, and I had neither the room nor the resources to deal with an aggressive dog. They then asked if I understood that meant Joey would have to be euthanized at the end of his quarantine. I did. Because he bit unprovoked, he was deemed a dangerous dog and the Shelter, by law, could not put him up for adoption. In a large city like Austin where the shelters have trained volunteers to work with dogs like Joey, it may have been a different story, but I'm pretty much it here. I could not put the other dogs at risk, nor myself, nor anyone in the community. It was hard to have to put Joey down, but it was the right thing to do under the circumstances. Sometimes we just have no choice. And it isn't easy.

To save Joey's sister, it seemed best to bring her to my property and keep her in one of the DAPS kennels. I live on the far end of town nearly at the end of the road. I have an acre and a half with no adjacent neighbors. To the west is an empty lot. Just past that is Jeannie and Bob. Jeannie is my executive director and the founder of DAPS. She also has DAPS dogs in permanent foster. If the dogs bark, we are the only ones close enough to be bothered.

Moving Josie to my place would make it easier to socialize her, get her in for spay, and find her a great home. She had other ideas. Steve and I set out immediately to try to catch the female who I would later name Josie in honor of her brother. I went home and grabbed a large crate, hot dogs, a slip leash, and collar. I thought the best way to catch Josie would be to place some high-value treats (think yummy) in the crate and when she entered to get them simply shut the door. This works more often than not, but the timing is absolutely critical. If the door is closed and the dog is not all the way in, they will push back and bolt. Most dogs are happy to jump in a vehicle and go for a ride, but the only time Josie had been in a car was to be dumped, and she had not forgotten that. She would not go near any car or truck. If we couldn't lure her into a crate, we might have to resort to trapping. I was very reluctant to trap as that would be another trauma that she wouldn't soon forget. All of the dogs that stay with me are crate trained. I know some people think it is cruel to crate, but if done correctly, the kennel or crate becomes the dog's den, and they seek it out. It offers them a sense of safety and of place, much like a den in the wild. The crate can never be used as punishment or abused by imprisoning a dog. That would, indeed, be cruel. I didn't want Josie afraid of the kennel too.

When we set out to catch Josie, we had to search to locate her. She had moved from Tommy's across the road, behind a house that belonged to friends of mine. I knocked on their door to let them know what we were doing and to ask permission to leave a crate in their field and allow us access to catch the dog. They were familiar with Josie as she had visited often. They were rescuers too, so they had no problem with our trying to rescue Josie on their property. They even asked what they could do to help. Ordinarily, I'd leave food for them to feed her, but we wanted her to be hungry to make the crate food more appealing. So I asked that for the time being, they do nothing. If they saw Josie, they could talk to her or toss treats in the crate but nothing beyond that. I really hoped we wouldn't be there very long. As we headed down their drive, it became evident that Josie was suspicious. She kept moving through the fields, we followed Josie wherever she went. She headed to the lower areas, then around the garage. We followed though it wasn't always easy! We had to climb over fences and stacked boxes or wire reels. Eventually, she came back up toward the driveway where we had the crate.

I needed to leave for an appointment in Taos, but Steve said he understood what needed to happen and that he was confident that he could handle it. I reminded him to be patient. We might not be able to catch her in one day. It may take several days to get her to trust the crate. Steve had used up most of the tripe, so I left him with the hot dogs and some cheese and wished him luck. A few hours later, Steve called to fill me in. He had gotten excited and closed the door too soon and lost Josie because of it. He said it was so close! All I could do was laugh. I could picture the scenario; Josie almost in, Steve behind the crate ready to slam the door shut at just the right instant, only it wasn't! The door hit Josie in the rear end which made her jump backward, shoving the door open and out of Steve's hand. It flew open, and she took off. That was our one chance for the crate to work. Josie would know now what we were up to. She was so smart! So we moved to plan "B."

Josie looked very much like Joey, but her personality was quite different. She was afraid though she was clearly not aggressive by nature and wanted to be close to me but was so wary. I knew it was due to abuse. We see this so often, too often. If she belonged to the owner we thought she did, we knew there was a young male who abused dogs in the home. That was going to be another challenging job, teaching her to trust after early abuse. I so hoped the crate incident didn't further her fear - too much. I was sure it made her warier, but it was a single quick incident so it might not have left a deep trauma. But it would have been a trauma no less. Joey had been far more confident and perhaps didn't receive the beatings she did. Every dog responds differently to physical abuse. Some become aggressive, others submissive, and some, like Josie, afraid. With time I can usually gain a dog's trust, but the wary ones are the hard ones. Sometimes it is actually very quickly that they realize I am different from the human that mistreated them. With others, it takes more time, and with some, they never fully trust humans again. Josie was afraid; she was also brilliant! Working and herding dogs have a greater awareness of their surroundings than other breeds. They have to if they are to control a herd. It is one reason why the crate didn't work, she probably knew exactly what Steve was up to. So for plan "B," I spent a few minutes every morning at Tommy's house down on 75 to train and socialize Josie. After losing Joey, I was determined to save Josie. One major challenge we'd have was the vehicle fear. If she was forced into a car or truck, she might not want to go with me. OK, that's putting it mildly. I was sure she would panic, which could be dangerous to both of us and my car. At first, she wouldn't let me very close. I was not surprised, but I was disappointed. I had hoped she would sense my calm and open heart, but I had been part of the crating plan, and she knew it! Since she had run feral for a couple of months, it was going to be a more significant challenge than with a dog who was not dumped to run free. Those two months meant that her basic wild instincts were what kept her alive. We have mountain lions and coyotes and other free-roaming dogs here, so she had to be smart, and she had to be fast to have survived on her own. Those months are also critical in the socialization of any puppy. That is when they learn to bond with humans, gain trust, learn to control their bite, potty train, and crate train. We had lost some serious ground. She and Joey probably helped each other survive during those two months. She may not have made it on her own without her brother. Now he was gone.

Anytime I have to work with a dog like Josie I go in with an open heart and project as much pure love their way as I can. I try not to have an agenda or time frame. I want to let the relationship evolve on its own time or the dog's time, not mine, and approach each on their terms. I fall in love with these dogs so easily. I feel a soul bond that I find difficult to put into words. But often, I am sure I know these souls. It is not an intellectual knowing but a heart knowing, a sense that we have been together before. I have great empathy for the abuse they have suffered at the hands of humans. I will never fathom how anyone can so abuse a puppy. A puppy who is here because of that human's failing. A simple spay would have prevented the litter. For the first week or more working with Josie, I sat under a large tree by the acequia (here in New Mexico we have an ancient irrigation system, a series of ditches, that runs through nearly every property in town. Dixon is very much a farming community. With an emphasis on organic farms.) just tossing treats her way. I didn't look at her, just sat facing the little orchard in Tommy's front yard. She would only snatch the treats that were a "safe" distance away.

Continuing to speak softly almost non-stop, hoping my tone of voice would have a calming effect and get her used to my presence and voice, I did this every day, often twice a day, for 15-30 minutes at a time. Sometimes Tommy and I would toss treats and talk to each other, just to be in her space. My interaction with Tommy would show her that he trusted me. Since he had been feeding Josie, she had begun to bond with him. She would even let him touch her. This gave me great hope. Tommy was retired so he could spend time with Josie daily. I was so grateful for his help and his love of animals. Elis, Tommy's next-door neighbor, and one of our new DAPS board members, was also working with her every day. With three of us interacting with her, we hoped Josie would trust quickly, but it soon wasn't looking as good as we had hoped. After a couple of weeks, she would sit nearer to me but just far enough that she was out of reach. I gave her treats and continued to talk in that rescuer's voice to her. I told her it was OK; that she was safe, that no one would hurt her anymore and that she was beautiful. And she was! I would attempt, very slowly, to get closer. I'd sit a few feet away offering treats and whispering to her. Often it was chilly in the morning - we weren't into full summer yet - so I'd sit in the sun but still close to her favorite spot by the tree. Later in the day, I would seek the shade. She would park herself about 4 feet away, a safe distance, but starting to come closer to take the treats. I held my hand out with a piece of hot dog or cheese or other yummy bit and just barely lifting my rear end off the ground, moved ever so slowly toward her.

At first, any movement caused her to back away, but I kept at it. I was not giving up on this girl! The progress was so slow, but progress nonetheless! I knew this had to happen on Josie's time, not mine. Day after day, we did this then finally after a couple of weeks, she took the treat from my hand and allowed me to scratch under her chin! I felt so relieved to finally make contact. I had tears in my eyes as she licked my hand. There was hope! When a dog is this cautious, I always wonder what they have been through. I really don't want to know the answer. I know enough to know it wasn't right. I didn't think knowing the details would change anything. All I could do was work with what I knew and sensed in her. Each day brought a bit more trust.

We moved from an under chin scratch to pats on the head. We started to work on "sit." She learned that in just minutes. I showed Tommy how I trained Josie on "sit" and "down" so that he could work with her during the day when he had time. We continued with her training and she started to roll over, so I encouraged that too. I still remember the first time she rolled over for a belly rub. A dog exposing their belly is a sign of trust and submission. She felt safe enough with me to expose her belly. I was ecstatic, and this was a huge step.

Finally, after many weeks, I could approach without her backing away, so it was time to introduce a collar. I left Tommy with a few collars and a slip leash. We left them just hanging or laying around so she would get used to them, play with them, even chew them. The leash really spooked her! Just holding it up for her to see or sniff made her nervous. I hoped having them around would lessen her fear.

Every day I sat on the stairs to be at the level of her head and offered her treats through the open collar or slip lead. After about a week of the head-through-the-collar (or slip lead) for-a-treat game, I slipped the wide-open leash around her neck. She went, berserk! She took off trying to outrun the bright pink lead. I sat quietly, not wanting to scare her more and just waited. It was a long wait! I couldn't see her through the trees and going after her would only make her run deeper into the thicket, so I waited. Slowly she reappeared. She came out of the bushes and just sat down. She was still frightened but also seemed to be a bit resigned. The leash was around her neck, and it was not pulled tight. I think that was when I felt I could breathe again. I called her over and offered treats, but she wouldn't come. She just sat in the driveway, looking scared and wanting that thing off.

This poor girl was scared of everything. I walked cautiously toward her telling her what a good girl she was. That it was OK. That I'd take it off. I expected her to bolt, but she just sat there frozen in place. I crouched down to her level as I made my final approach. She stayed right there. I gave her treats as I very carefully removed the leash. She licked my face and stayed close so I could

Josie 🐾

rub her and reassure her that it was all right. I took a breath of relief. And so did Josie.

Each day we repeated the same desensitization routine. Put the leash on and take the leash off, over and over so she would see it wasn't quite as scary as she perceived it to be. We did this for another week. Day by day Josie was less concerned about it. We switched to a collar. At first, I kept it wide open, putting it on and taking it off. Finally, I put it on and left it on. Not fully tight yet but tight enough that it wouldn't fall off. She pawed at it only briefly. Over the next few days, I would tighten it to where it should be; she no longer seemed concerned. That was a huge victory!

With a collar on, we could start leash training. As you can imagine, she hated being on a leash. She thrashed and pulled and tried to get it off. I backed up and just draped the leash across her back. I have worked with several dogs who just don't like being on a leash. Many of them do much better with a harness, it feels less constricting or threatening.

She was pretty good with the harness, but I was the only one who could put it on her. (Still now, a year and a half later I am the only one who can get a harness on her. We are now training almost every day, so I hope she will allow Jeannie to harness her soon.) Now, when I headed over to Tommy's, whether I was in my car or in the rescue truck, she would come running as soon as she heard me coming. We had made great progress! She was more and more social. Some times Tommy would leave his front door open, and she would invite herself in! The cats weren't so sure about that, but she didn't seem to care much about the cats, so it remained fairly calm.

Josie was now about five months old, and at six months, we were expecting that she would go into her first heat. (Heat is the time during which a female or bitch is fertile. Since Josie was an outdoor dog, every male for a three-mile radius would know she was in heat!) I was stepping up the training to get her in for spay before then so we didn't have a litter. I love whelping puppies. It is one of the most incredible and beautiful experiences I have had in rescue. The work of feeding and cleaning up after a litter is a full-time job, both for the mom and the foster mom-me. Josie needed to be spayed soon. So it was time to introduce her to "going for a ride." For the next few weeks, much of our training time was spent just sitting in the backseat of my car. Sometimes it was the front seat of my car, whichever Josie was in the mood for. At first, she would only sit outside the car and wait for me to give her a treat. Then she put her paws on the front seat, but that was it, she wasn't coming in, no way no how. Eventually, she climbed into the passenger seat! I could see the concern in her eyes and on her face. She is very expressive. But she did it anyway. Again huge!

Then I closed the door. She looked at me with fear in her eyes. I waited. I didn't start the car I just wanted her in the enclosed space. I stroked her and talked to her, telling her she would stay with me, that I would not abandon her. I told her we needed to go to the vet. We continued for another week or so, just sitting in the car. It was now deep into summer and I was starting to get very concerned about Josie going into heat. With great trepidation, I decided to start the car. She didn't move. Wow. I put it in gear and slowly moved ten feet. She panicked and flew into the hatchback, trying to escape. This was not good, clearly, getting her comfortable with riding in a car was not going to be easy. I wasn't defeated, yet, but I was really getting concerned that I would not be able to get her to the vet for a spay. Our local vet could take care of all of her shots at Tommy's, but we couldn't spay outside the clinic. I'm sure many would have lost their patience by now, but I knew that would get me nowhere. I wasn't giving up, but she certainly was teaching me patience.

As I was driving home in the afternoon of August 2nd, I caught a glimpse of Josie across the street from Tommy's and down the road a little bit near where we had tried crating her. Josie wasn't alone. She was with one of the unfixed males that wander around town. The two dogs were standing facing in opposite directions. "Did I just see what I think I saw?" "Please, no! " I yelled at the windshield. I turned around and went back to the dogs. Sure enough, they were "locked" in the mating position. Josie looked embarrassed or concerned. I admit it, I took photos. I had not seen any sign of her being in heat, but clearly, she was. Many thoughts ran through my head like; it was her first heat, so maybe it wouldn't take? Wishful thinking at best, he was an older dog, so perhaps he had a low sperm count? Not sure it works that way in dogs. Was there anything I could have done to prevent this? Why isn't that dog neutered? (I know the answer.) There was nothing I could do about it now, so I waited for them to unhook to be sure Josie was OK. I do think she was a bit sore and I wondered if Josie understood what had just happened. I suspected she did but had no clue what would result from it. I knew she would be a good mom, but that wasn't a good enough reason for her to be a mom. So now time, was, indeed, of the essence. We could spay very early in the pregnancy, so I only had a couple of weeks to get Josie in for spay, or we would be having puppies.

We set several different kinds of crates and kennels out at Tommy's house, hoping that Josie would choose a crate and have her puppies in it. Since Josie was still pretty much feral, she probably would find a hiding place rather than use a crate anyway. I would do all I could to keep that from happening though. The concern was that if she had the puppies in the woods, she would lose them to predators or, as it got colder at night, hypothermia. It would also be much harder to socialize them and their momma. Losing the ground we had made would be tragic. I continued trying to get her to go for a ride so we could get her to the vet. I kept an eye on her belly, looking for the telltale signs of pregnancy. Four weeks in when I was just getting her into the car, there were still no signs of pregnancy. I checked her every day. She just wasn't showing. Then, at six weeks - boom! Suddenly her belly rounded, her teats enlarged, oh yeah she was pregnant. It was time to switch gears and prepare for her being a mom. Now clearly pregnant she was probably due in about two weeks. Since I witnessed the coupling, I had a pretty good idea of when she was due. Canine gestation is 58-68 days. We were closing in on the end of September and puppies would be due the first week of October. Tommy and I started setting up nesting spots for Josie, large fluffy dog beds under the tree, other soft bedding in the doghouse, in a crate, all the places she liked to hang out during the day all now had a warm place to whelp. We placed treats in each bed, hoping to convince her that it was safe. She showed no interest in our accommodations. We were disappointed but not surprised. So we watched, and we waited.

On Tuesday afternoon, October 3rd, I went to check on Josie as I had been since the mating. She was full-bellied and in milk so due anytime. She ran up the driveway, as usual, to greet me and receive treats and love. Well, she didn't run so much, as waddled now. She sat down and let me pet her for approximately three seconds before she stood up, tucked her tail, and her usually prick ears went flat. They stuck straight out sideways, which made her look a lot like Yoda. I turned to Tommy and said, "Oh, this isn't good." "I think she's going into hiding to whelp." With her natural instincts kicking in, I watched her skulk down the driveway. I followed her as I sensed she was going to hide. She knew the puppies were coming and she was going to find a safe place to have them. I desperately wanted to know where! She went down Tommy's long driveway and across highway 75. I followed at a distance, so I didn't cause her to run, but had to stop to let a car go by. After it passed, she was gone. She just disappeared! The property across the street had many places in which she could hide. I looked and looked but could not find her. I checked the drainage culvert that ran under the road, but the opening seemed too small, and there was a spider web across the mouth so she couldn't have entered there. I called her to come, but she did not. It was late in the day, it was getting cold and dark, stormy weather was moving in later in the week, so I went home. Tommy would keep an eye out as she would be getting hungry and most likely would come to him for food.

Had Josie had her pups? I didn't know but her behavior the previous afternoon was a pretty good indication that she was very close. It was a cold, grey, damp October morning. By afternoon the sun would usually warm the day but perhaps not this day. I started my search at Tommy's calling Josie to come. She had learned recall and was generally prompt to come when called, but no Josie. If she had just whelped, she would not leave her pups, but I hoped she'd give me a yelp or bark in response to my calls. I moved across the street, continuing to call her name. As I rounded the corner by the front door, I heard a kitten cry. There was a tree right out in front of the door. A thorough search of the tree for the crying kitten yielded nothing. Then it cried again. It sounded like it was behind me. I was facing the tree with my back to the door. I turned. Behind me was an adobe abutment next to the front door. I thought perhaps a kitten had gotten lodged between the screen door and the wooden front door. The screen was locked from the inside but was loose enough that I could peek inside…no kitten. I heard it again! The sound was bouncing off the adobe house, so it was hard to pinpoint the source. My heart was starting to race. Was this dog rescue now going to include a kitten? I looked down so that my vision wasn't influencing how I heard the sound, and right there… under the flagstone overhang of the doorstep… right next to my foot…. wedged behind the dried stems of some kind of old dead plant… lay a puppy!! I caught my breath. A puppy!! A beautiful tiny newborn puppy!! It sounded just like a kitten! I could so easily have missed it, wedged out of view under the step. Wow. Amazing! Josie had gone into labor here in the yard! I tried to slide the puppy out, but it was wedged so tightly between the stems of the woody plant and the flagstone step that I couldn't get it to move in either direction. It was continually crying now. It was probably still wet and slippery when it wiggled in, not knowing where it was. (Puppies are born with their eyes sealed shut. The eyes and ears require two weeks after birth to finish developing. At two weeks, the eyes open but should not be exposed to bright light for another couple of weeks as their vision continues to progress.) I didn't want to injure the tiny pup, so I quickly snapped off the plant stems and pulled the puppy free. This pup could not have crawled far being a newborn. It was possible Josie was bringing her back to her den and had another contraction, dropping the puppy as she ran to her hiding place to finish whelping the litter. This tiny pup was a girl, and she looked just like her daddy! Black and tan but with speckled white forelegs like Josie. She was cold as a stone, but she was alive!! And she was strong. Barely a half-pound, but healthy and well-muscled. Josie had been well fed for her entire pregnancy to be sure the pups were born healthy. I did a quick search of the area, but there was no sac, no placenta. Her umbilical cord had been chewed, and she had been thoroughly cleaned. The remaining umbilical cord was still wet, so she was less than an hour old. Most likely, less than 30 minutes old based on how damp she was. She was probably the firstborn. I whipped around to see if Josie was anywhere close by. She wasn't. I searched for any other abandoned puppies. Thankfully there were none. I called Adele who offered to bring puppy milk replacer ASAP. You can always count on Adele in an emergency. She generally kept puppy milk replacer in her freezer for just this kind of emergency. This baby would be well fed despite her circumstances!

Often young mothers don't quite know what to do when they go into labor. It's all new and pretty scary. What I have witnessed is that the first birth is quite painful and comes as a surprise to the mother. After the first is born, the momma settles into the rhythm of labor. Particularly with their first puppy, if they are not close to the whelping box or den they'll just drop them and leave them still in the sac. Those puppies usually don't survive unless there is human intervention. Sometimes the instinct doesn't kick in with the first puppy, and without intervention, they die. Josie knew to open the sac, clean the pup, and eat the placenta. The mother dog eats the placenta for several reasons. One is, so there is no bloody debris lying about to attract predators. Another is that is it super nutritious and will give her sustenance to whelp the remaining pups.

This little girl would be Xena but with a Z. (We generally name litters with the same first letter. I was going to have a tough time coming up with more than a few "X" names!) She was, after all, a warrior. Tucked safely into my tank top she could rest and be warm. Hearing and feeling my heartbeat would give her some comfort. I rushed home to get my puppy milk replacer and start bottle-feeding her as quickly as possible. Unfortunately, having been left behind, she was not going to get the colostrum from her mother, which is so vital for building her immunity. The puppy milk replacer would probably save her life, though, good enough! I headed back to the place I found Zena, Josie had to be close! I called and called; nothing.

I searched for 4 1/2 hours and couldn't find her. I'd covered acres. Tromped through brambles and high dry grass looking for any clue. By then, I was bleary-eyed and almost unable to take another step. My head ached, and thinking was difficult. I had to give up for the day. I checked in with Tommy, he reported that he had not seen her. We put food out in her usual spot on the porch so she could eat when she felt safe enough to leave the litter, or hungry enough. I was exhausted from very little sleep and a high-intensity search in the cold and damp. I too was hungry, so I took Zena home, keeping her warm in a bed of soft blankets and microwavable puppy warming pads. She needed to be fed every two hours, and though I carried a bottle during the search, a quiet meal at home would do us both good.

Zena was incredibly strong, a good nurser, and by the next day, she was eliminating on her own. That was remarkable! Usually, for the first week or two, the mother dog has to stimulate the puppies to pee and poop by licking them after feeding. This also keeps the puppies and the whelping box clean. Zena just peed and pooped on her own, in my shirt, but I was OK with that! When I fed her at home, we did the usual feeding and stimulating with a warm, wet cotton ball, but she seemed to already have it down. Zena was doing great, but I was very concerned about that rough start. If she had gotten too cold, she might not survive. She continued to eat well throughout the night and slept well between feedings. Me? Not so much. How did I happen to be there just minutes after Josie dropped her? I don't know. Where were Josie and the rest of the puppies? I didn't know that, either! What had I missed? I had to stop questioning and just accept that my tiny little fighter was going to be all right. The rest of the litter had their mom, so they would all be safe and well-fed. I was exhausted but elated.

The next morning, still bleary-eyed and drop-dead exhausted I was determined to find Josie and her other pups. This tiny puppy needed her mother after all! I headed back out with my dog Blondie in tow. Blondie was a shepherd mix, possibly part coyote, and she loved puppies. I thought if anybody could find Josie and the rest of the litter it would be Blondie. We searched for another 2 1/2 hours, no sign, no sound. We searched all of the places I had the previous day, nothing. I kept coming back and looking at that culvert, under the road at the end of Tommy's driveway.

I told Tommy and Elis that at some point she would have to come out for food, and then we could find the puppies. It was a damp and dreary day, we were all tired, frustrated, and concerned. Zena and I went home.

Jennifer, one of our other board members, called to see how things were going. I filled her in, nearly in tears from exhaustion. She asked if she could take Zena for the night to help out and give me a break. Besides, she too was an experienced rescuer, and having a newborn puppy to take care of really is a pretty fantastic thing. She and her teenage daughter, Leela, could tag team on feedings, and I could pick Zena up at Yoga class in the morning. Jennifer is a gifted Yoga instructor, and our Yoga time together has seen us both through difficult times, including divorce. Jennifer and Leela came by right after the call, and I handed Zena off. It was such a relief to get a break for the night, but I wondered how long we'd have to bottle feed. If we couldn't find Josie soon, we'd have to schedule feeders to take Zena, so no one was too overburdened.

In the morning at yoga class Jennifer, looking a little fried herself, handed Zena back to me. She hadn't anticipated how hard the every two hours feeding schedule was going to be! She loved it, but . . . we had a good laugh. Each having a complete understanding of how challenging it is to be sleep-deprived after such a nurturing and beautiful night saving an abandoned puppy. After yoga, we planned to continue the search. Having a few more people might bring a

Josie 🐾

better result. For the next hour and a half, we focused on asanas (yoga positions), a lovely break from the work and worry of puppies! While lying in savasana, the rest period at the end of class, there was a knock on the glass. The yoga studio has tall glass doors, and before I even opened an eye and knew who it was!! I sat up as Jennifer went to the door. Sure enough, it was Tommy and Elis. They were so excited! They had to hunt me down. Knowing I did Yoga on Friday mornings but not sure where, they drove all over Dixon and happened to see my car parked where we held class. Jennifer got up more quickly than I could and opened the door just enough to poke her head out. Tommy apologized profusely for interrupting class and asked if he could talk to me. They had found Josie! Jennifer said, "Oh, you can always interrupt this class for puppies!!"

Elis had been searching for Josie but was hungry, so she had gone to the Co-op to grab a breakfast sandwich of egg and cheese. As she enjoyed her breakfast, she walked the property thinking, precisely as I had, that Josie *must* be close. But where could she have hidden?! As she walked, she called "Josie, Josie! " When suddenly Josie poked her nose out of her hiding place, grabbed the sandwich, and disappeared back inside. Inside the culvert under the highway!! The one with the spider webs! "No way! " I thought. How could that be?" I grabbed my yoga stuff and ran. As I left Jennifer asked if I needed her help. I said, "Yes, please! Come as soon as you can."

We headed over to Tommy's to figure out what to do. I let Jeannie know that Operation Puppy Rescue (that made it sound official) was now in full swing! I called Adele on my way over as she has a lot of rescue experience, and I was going to need her help. I asked that everyone give Josie space. A new mom can be VERY protective. I didn't want anyone bitten nor did I want to scare Josie or make her feel threatened by a crowd. We were only a small crowd, but more would gather soon. Tommy and I approached, and Josie poked her head out from the culvert. Tommy told me he had gotten close when they first found her. He had just wanted to say hello when Josie snapped at him. She bit him but did not break the skin.

He was crestfallen because she was as much his dog is anyone's; he didn't understand why she didn't like him anymore. I felt bad. He was so sweet and so kind to her, but I wasn't really surprised. I explained that she was just being a good mom protecting her babies. I then sat down on the embankment at the end of the culvert to see what Josie would do with me that close. She came out cautiously but when she saw that it was me excitedly wiggled into my lap, kissed my face, let me pet her for just a second, and then went back to her babies. She was beaming with pride! I said, "Tommy, I can't explain this. She has spent far more time with you than with me, but like I told you before, there's something about me that makes her feel safe." This has happened over and over. And it is both a blessing and a burden.

Adele, who arrived right after Josie returned to the culvert, has been a volunteer for DAPS for decades. She's always there when you need her! Adele was also a volunteer firefighter here in Dixon for years. She's quick on her feet, she has a lot of rescue experience, far more than I have, and she's excellent for moral support. I was so glad to have her help. Adele and I chatted for a few minutes deciding our best course of action. We needed to get this litter out now as the culvert Josie had chosen was on a runoff ditch, and there was a severe storm moving in! We had what is referred to as "monsoon season." It usually began in July and ran into September. Afternoon thunderstorms that brought inches of rain in a matter of minutes. The local arroyos would become raging rivers at times! Flash floods, daily. This year they were still happening in October. Not unheard of but not the norm either. If we didn't get the puppies out, they would be swept away and most likely drown. I went home to get the truck and a trap or two.

At DAPS, we have a whole collection of traps. Everything from mouse size to large dog and we've used them all. I debated with myself, "Do I take the small dog size, or do I take the large dog size?" They both would not fit in the truck at the same time, had to make a decision right or wrong. I didn't live that far front the center of town, but every minute counted! I opted for the smaller one because it would fit into the ditch in front of the culvert and was big enough for Josie. The large trap was far too big for the ditch. We had decided the best thing would be to trap Josie so no one would get bitten while we removed the pups. Our options were limited. If we could trap her, everyone would be safe, and she could be transported in the trap and moved to my guest bathroom, a.k.a. the whelping room. There the mother and pups would be safe and warm until they were old enough to move out to the outdoor kennel.

Yoga clothes were not going to work for this job so I changed into hiking gear that was made of nylon fabric figuring it would be the thinnest and most slippery for sliding into the culvert. I returned with the trap, and we placed it in the ditch at the end of the pipe. The trap wouldn't fit. Tommy ran up to his garage and grabbed a shovel. He started digging to widen the ditch. I watched to see if Josie was getting anxious and looking to see what was going on. I didn't see her. In just a couple of minutes, we had the trap in place. That was one of those moments, and I have them fairly often, where I think, "I love this community! " People just jump in and get the job done. Tommy helped placed the trap as close to the culvert as possible without risking the door hanging up on it. We didn't want Josie to have the option of moving past it when she came out but too close, and the trap wouldn't spring. There was some space between the trap and the culvert, but I didn't think she'd leave the pups and we had moved people far enough away (a crowd had now gathered on the far side of the road) that she shouldn't have felt threatened by their presence. With everyone clear on the plan, it was time to set the trap. We'd have one chance, maybe two if we were extraordinarily fortunate but I hoped not to find out if I was right on that.

Everyone needed to be very quiet while we set the trap. If this didn't work, we didn't have a back-up plan and, we were running out of time. Josie was so smart we had one chance to get it done. Zena was placed in the back of the trap. I had very mixed feelings about using the puppy as bait, but my hunch was that Josie, knowing she had left her firstborn behind, would be anxious to be reunited. I was getting concerned that Zena had been without for too long. This needed to happen now so Zena could nurse. I also moved away so Josie wouldn't be so suspicious. Zena had her role down! She soon started to cry, loudly! Josie came out of the culvert. But she looked at the trap, she looked at Zena, and then she looked at me to say "No way am I going in there! " And she ducked back inside the pipe. You could feel the energy drop. Not defeated, just disappointed, Adele and I conferred. We agreed that perhaps the small trap was too intimidating for Josie. I pulled Zena out, stuck her back in my shirt, tossed the trap aside (we'd put it at the other end of the culvert as a second possibility) and headed back to switch it out for the big one. The bigger trap was huge but might not intimidate Josie like the smaller version. As suspected, the large trap would not fit into the ditch where the small one had been. One look at Tommy and he started digging. Again he made the trench wide enough in no time at all! I was so impressed. Tommy is a pretty laid back guy, but he just jumped on it! I put Zena in the back of the massive trap, and we moved away. It was now Saturday afternoon, and a powerful storm was coming in. If we had a deluge, this drainage culvert would be a river, and the puppies would drown. Time was of the essence, and I was dog tired. This rescue needed to happen now!

Zena was in the large trap now and starting to make a lot of noise. I had purposely skipped a feeding so that she would make more noise and now that she knew her mother was near she was ramping up. Puppies need to eat every couple of hours, but if she had been fed and were quiet, this would never have worked. Granted, it felt cruel to not keep to the feeding schedule, but sometimes the decisions we have to make are tough. I would never let Zena get to the point of so hungry that it would be dangerous, but I had to keep her hungry for the benefit of the litter. Thankfully Zena didn't have to wait long for lunch to arrive! Her escalating cry, now more of a howl, brought Josie out of the culvert and the more massive trap didn't intimidate her. She didn't even hesitate! Once the trap door slammed down, Josie shot me a look. I hoped this would not cause the loss of the trust I had built, but I knew that was a possibility. Then she looked down at her first puppy with such love in her eyes and gave me a very different look. This one said, "You found her! Thank you." I thought I might have just earned a few points!

With Zena and Josie both in the trap, we loaded it into the truck. Zena could nurse while we pulled the other pups. I hadn't paid much attention to what was going on around the trapping. I now saw the small crowd that had gathered near the far end of the pipe. I asked everyone to stay back so that we could get the puppies out as quickly as possible. Down in the ditch and in a hurry, I didn't notice that the channel had been bent in. Entering the opening, I promptly smacked my forehead on the point. I wasn't mortally wounded so I tucked my head to slide into the 18-inch culvert.

I should've fit in easily. I'm not very big, although my shoulders are almost 18 inches wide. I was a competitive swimmer, so they are broad, especially for a woman. It would be tight, but I thought I'd fit. But since the culvert was half full of silt from storms over the years, it was too snug. I made it in up to about my waist and got stuck. Great. This was a major snag. I was going to need a smaller person's help.

While I was in the pipe, I had assessed the situation. There, about 20 feet in, was the pile of puppies. Not quite halfway under the road. Probably five or six of them. About 15 feet from me was one dead puppy. I had tossed my chimney brush in the truck thinking it might be useful for pulling puppies out if they were reasonably close to the end of the culvert, but it wasn't long enough to reach the pile of pups. It was just long enough to reach the dead one. Since I was going to have to send someone else in, I pulled the dead puppy and wrapped him up for later burial. He was flat. Josie probably rolled over on him while she was nursing. This is something that happens pretty often. The mother doesn't realize a puppy is underneath her, and they are essentially suffocated. It was unfortunate. But there was no time to think about that now, we needed to get the other pups out and soon.

As I was thinking about what to do next, Haven showed up with his iPad to videotape the rescue effort. Haven was the grandson of Michele, the woman who had been bitten by Josie's brother. "What are you doing?" Haven asked. "We're rescuing puppies that were born in this culvert. Except I don't fit so I can't get the puppies out." I replied. "Rowan would fit! " Haven said with enthusiasm. Rowan is Haven's little brother. Haven was only 11 or 12, but he was a big kid. Rowan, at nine, was still pretty small. "Would he go in there?" I asked as Haven looked at the culvert. "Sure," Haven replied. "So you are giving up your little brother to go into a culvert under the highway to rescue puppies?" I asked, uncertain that this was a good idea. "Yup." He said without hesitation. "OK Haven where is Rowan?" I inquired. "He's at the library. I was just going to get them when I saw you," came Haven's reply. "OK, go get him! " I said excitedly. The Library was just up the road, and they were back in no time! While we waited, I made double sure there was no imminent danger in the culvert like spiders or snakes. The boys arrived in little time out of breath from running. Rowan was your typical flaxen-haired, wiry nine-year-old boy. He and his buddy Miles came trotting up. Miles was also thin but had broad shoulders so I was pretty sure he'd have the same experience I did, wiggle in part way and get stuck. So rather than chance it and waste more time I'd have Rowan do the culvert, and Miles be my extra hands with puppies. I turned to them and asked, "Are you willing to crawl into this culvert to save a litter of puppies?" "Sure!" they shrugged in unison. I had been far enough into the culvert with a powerful flashlight to know there was nothing dangerous in there. Since it was a drainage culvert, it was washed out quite frequently. I removed the dead puppy before the boys got there so that they didn't have to see it. So, as big brother Haven videotaped, Rowan wiggled in and grabbed two puppies. He shimmied backward until I could grab his feet at which point I told him to tuck his head and not sit up until I told him he was clear. I did not want him to hit the back of his head on the point on that culvert. The boys needed to remain safe and unharmed. We did this three times, wiggled in, wiggled out, waited for the all-clear. He brought out six fat healthy puppies, handed them to Miles who gave them to me to check out and put in their carrier. In total there were five girls and one boy. The puppy that died was also a boy.

Rowan and Miles were curious about the dead pup and asked if they could see him. They wanted to know what had happened, how had he died. We talked about how mother dogs sometimes roll or sit on a puppy while nursing and they don't realize it. I suspected that was the case with this little guy. He looked otherwise healthy. They thought it was kind of sad. I agreed but said, "Look, you saved the other six. Thank you! "

I was wearing my favorite DAPS cap, an embroidered black stonewashed, cotton baseball cap. I took it off, and I put it on Rowan's head saying, "Rowan, you are now an honorary board member of the Dixon Animal Protection Society. This is my favorite DAPS cap, I want you to have it." He held the brim in his hand. While the cap sat on his head, a look of pride spread on his face. Then his expression changed. He looked at me and asked, "This is your favorite?" "Yeah, it is," I replied. "Then I don't want it. You should keep it," he stated. This nine-year-old boy had this kind of compassion. I have often said the children in this community are extraordinary! With tears in my eyes, I thanked Rowan and asked what he might like instead. "Nothing," he said as he and Miles took off up the road. Just an ordinary day in Dixon, New Mexico! I turned to Haven and handed him a $20 bill. I asked him to give it to the boys as a thank you. Perhaps they could all go buy something together. He said he would, and I am sure he did.

During the next few days, when I was out and about at the Co-op, at the Post Office, a few people commented on the rescue. They had been there to watch, and we're so very grateful that we saved these puppies. Just another day in Dixon but it was a day that reminded me just how unique our community was.

I had no idea these people were there. I knew people had gathered, but I had no idea who they were. My focus was on saving the puppies and keeping the kids safe! We accomplished both. So Josie and the puppies and I headed home. For the first two weeks, they would make my guest bathroom their home. I sat for hours and just watched and listened to the puppies nursing. Though not an unusual occurrence by any stretch it was still awe-inspiring and so beautiful to watch Josie be such a perfect mom. Admittedly I am a puppy breath addict. That sweet smell, the warm fat little bodies in my hands, to me, this is nirvana. It wouldn't last, so I relished every minute I could. Once their eyes opened and they became mobile, they moved to the outdoor kennel. The amount of puppy mess from a litter this size was mind-boggling. Just minutes after cleaning the tub, it was covered with poo once again. Josie wasn't terribly comfortable being locked inside either. So once mobile and eliminating on their own out they went. It was fall and getting cooler but wouldn't be terribly cold for a while yet. Being part husky they would all have thick undercoats to keep them warm. We set up an outdoor kennel covered in tarps so that Josie would feel safe and secure. I had an igloo doghouse, and as it got a cooler in late fall, we insulated it with straw and wool blankets. All curled up with momma during the night the puppies were very cozy. All of the puppies were given Z names; Zena, Zsa Zsa, Zenobia, Zelda, Zinnia and Zachary, the only male to survive. Zena, Zenobia, and Zelda all had markings like their dad, black and tan with some speckling. Zsa Zsa, Zinnia, and Zachary all had Josie's coloring but different markings. Josie is about half white and half red with splotches and speckles all over. These three were more solid red with white accent markings like forehead blazes, neck stripes, and white feet. I worked with the puppies every day; handling them, petting them, socializing them, so that when it came time, they would be ready for their new homes. Josie continued to be extremely protective of her puppies. No one except me could go anywhere near their kennel without her snarling and barking. It took weeks before she accepted Jeannie's presence. At times, when I couldn't get back from teaching in Santa Fe, or I was out of town, Jeannie had to feed them. That is not easy with a fiercely protective momma dog, but she managed to feed Josie and the pups and not get bitten. With time, as Josie mellowed into the routine, it became easier. She stopped being so protective and allowed Jeannie in, to see the puppies, and visit with her. During the early weeks with the puppies, I gave Josie a break from her training. She needed to be with the litter and focus on being a mom. But I had real concerns that if she had any complications, I would not be able to get her to the vet with her total aversion to vehicles. As if on cue, she developed mastitis, my fear became a reality. How was I to get her to the vet? Dr. Kim, our local Veterinarian, was not available, and the mastitis was severe. Josie was in pain from the infected milk ducts. Her teats were red, hot, and swollen. I'd have to use the pups as bait again. I felt awful about doing it, but with severe mastitis, the puppies would not be allowed to nurse. They were still too young to wean, so we had to supplement with bottle feeding until Josie felt better. But that wouldn't be until after we started antibiotics after we got her to the vet - if we got her to the vet. The puppies were loaded into an airline crate. The weather was cool enough that a wire crate in the back of the DAPS truck, even with a cap, would be pretty chilly. The plastic crate might feel more like the igloo and offer more protection and security. With the pups in, Josie jumped right in! Wow! Progress?? Adele helped me load the truck, and we headed to the Cottonwood Vet Clinic.

Josie, as expected, had severe mastitis. The puppies were weighed and recorded while we had them there. Everyone enjoyed meeting the family and oohing and aahing over the beautiful pups. Josie was on alert! She watched her pups the entire time but showed no aggression. That was a huge relief! With everyone checked out and medication prescribed, it was time to go. Or not. Puppies in the crate were now of no interest to Josie. I was afraid it would only work once. This is one smart dog! Josie ran under the truck and hunkered down. No amount of yummy treats of any kind made the slightest impression. Josie was not coming out. We tried putting the crate down low so she could walk right in rather than jump up into the truck bed. Not happening. I tried begging, pleading, crying, crawling under with her to comfort her, but nothing made her move. So there I sat, next to the truck, leaning against the filthy tire, alone, exhausted and out of ideas. The puppies were getting hungry (so was I. I hadn't thought to bring food. If I don't eat I experience low blood sugar, so I was fading fast) and vocal, but even that didn't have any effect on momma Josie. She was staying under the truck, period. Debbie, the fabulous receptionist, came out to see what was up. She'd noticed the truck was still sitting in the lot. It was lunchtime at the vet, they are closed for lunch, so we'd been there for about an hour. I was starting to think we'd be there until nightfall and I was falling asleep. Debbie looked at my predicament and laughed. "Did you try treats?" she asked. "Yup, all out," I replied. "Hmmm, let me see what I've got," she said as she went back in. Seconds later, she emerged with a small plastic container of what looked like a dip. It was an odd brown color. Not the sort of thing that I would consider eating or giving to my dog! "What is that?" I asked. "Ground roast beef and mayo dip," she said with enthusiasm. "It's delicious!" She tried to convince me, the vegetarian, I wasn't convinced! She leaned over and let Josie, who was still under the pickup, have a whiff. Holy smokes! That got her attention! Josie came out and took a taste. I guess it was good! Debbie tossed the container into the crate, and Josie jumped in after it! I slammed that door so hard it startled us all!! Josie turned and looked toward the noise and went back to licking the dip as the pups gathered for their lunch from momma.

At eight weeks our local vet Dr. Kim came over and gave the puppies their first shots and their first full examination. They were all plump and healthy and ready for adoption. Josie was a stellar mom but clearly wanted to be done. I scheduled a transfer through Stray Hearts in Taos. The puppies would go to Colorado, where they had a good chance of finding loving homes. Zachary was adopted locally by a friend, a single dad with a three-year-old son, he is now called Milo. The day they arrived to pick up Zachary, Elijah was not a happy boy. It was past nap time, and it was abundantly clear. While his dad and I talked about the adoption and what they would need to do; like have him neutered, continue with the puppy shot schedule, etc. I said, "Donny, why don't you just give Zachary to Elijah, let him hold him?" Elijah instantly stopped crying and just beamed. Zachary sat in Elijah's lap and licked his face. That was one of those absolutely beautiful moments in which I knew it would be a perfect adoption for both of them. Elijah, a redhead, even had the same hair color as Zachary, now Milo. Eli looked at Milo with the sweetest expression! A boy and his dog.

The day the other puppies were scheduled for transfer to Colorado Puppy Rescue Zena became very ill. She had watery, bloody diarrhea, and was vomiting. Classic signs of Parvo but she didn't have the lethargy that comes with Parvo. I immediately took her to Cottonwood, and of course, the first test they wanted to do was for Parvovirus. It was negative. I asked to test for Giardia too, so we did. It was not just positive, it was positive very quickly. That meant a high level of infection. So at least we knew what we were dealing with. It was contagious but not nearly as infectious as Parvo. A round of Metronidazole was all she needed, and she was healthy in a couple of days. None of the other puppies had it, but I called to postpone the transfer just in case. It turned out that they needed to put the litter off a week anyway. I love it when things work that way! They do so many transfers, but they often run out of space. I pondered how Zena was sick, but the others weren't. Would they break with it while we waited? I hoped not. Zena had escaped the kennel one day and possibly ate something she shouldn't, but I also wondered if she had a less robust immune system from being abandoned and not able to nurse those first critical hours. None of the others got sick and transferred the next week. So the puppies left in stages; first Zach, then the rest of the litter except Zena and Zenobia, which I think was really good for Josie. It has to be incredibly traumatic for a mother dog to see her puppies just disappear.

I kept Zenobia with Zena while she went through her antibiotic treatment so that Josie could get used to the idea of the puppies going away and so that Zena had a buddy. Zenobia was the shy one and rather than her shyness getting better with time and handling it had worsened. I was concerned it might be a problem with prospective adopters. Having her stay with Zena I could then concentrate my socializing on just two puppies. Having that one-on-one time really brought Zenobia out of her shell. What matters is that she gained confidence during the two weeks after the others transferred. Once Zena was done with her treatment, they went on transfer together. Josie seemed perfectly content with the puppies being gone.

Josie and I picked up training where we left off. I was able to finally crate her! It took weeks, but she was crate trained enough that I could get her in the kennel and down to the vet. I dropped her off for spay, ran some errands, and headed back home. Just as I was coming down my road, I received a phone call from the vet asking how soon I could return to the clinic, they could not get Josie out of her crate. I knew she didn't much like her kennel yet and had assumed that as soon as they open the door, she would be happy to be free. I was wrong! I sat by the crate, and when I opened the door, Josie crawled right into my lap. We gave her the anesthetic while I held her.

Both alert and willful, they do not like to lose control, and going under makes them feel like they are losing control. I stayed with Josie while we put the mask on for the gas, the second phase of surgery anesthesia. She fought that too. When she was finally out, I left. But before I left, I asked that she be put back in the crate while still under anesthesia. I knew if they didn't, I was not going to get her there in this lifetime! I went back and picked her up late in the afternoon and brought her home. She was so happy to be out of that crate. (And she has never gone back in. Not that crate, not any crate.) It was now too cold outside for her to be in the outdoor kennel. She is now with the older dogs in the studio kennel set up with the heater and her crate. I still have hope that she will one day use the crate. The studio kennel has a sizable indoor room that I use for storage and a dog door out to an outdoor enclosure so she can go in and out as she needs to. She lives with an older chocolate Chihuahua that we think was dumped; we never found his owner. And my Schnauzer mix with the head injury. The head injury makes her snappy and unpredictable with people, but she is fine with other dogs, so the three of them are kennel mates. When I am in the studio, they hang out with me.

Greetings with Love From a Lonely Dog
by Peter Anthony Kirkup

I wish someone would tell me
what it is that I've done wrong.
Why do I have to stay chained up
and be left alone so long?
they seemed so glad to have me
when I came here as a pup.
There were so many things we'd do
while I was growing up.
The Master said he'd train me
as a companion and a friend.
The mistress said she'd never fear
to be left alone again . . .

Ginny

In awe, I lifted the tiny puppy to look at his face. "Wyatt!" I said aloud. "Your name will be 'Wyatt!'" I repeated as I looked at my fellow rescuer Katie. "I don't know why 'Wyatt.'" I told her. It usually takes me a while to name a new rescue, but "Wyatt" hit me like a palm slap to the forehead - bam! When something like that happens, I no longer question it; just go with it. Both Mark and Katie said they liked it. So "Wyatt" it was. But, what to call his mom?

As Mark and I drove back to my place, where Wyatt and his mom would be fostered, I looked up Wyatt Earp, the only Wyatt I knew, on my iPhone. Earp's mother's name was Virginia, but that just didn't fit this girl. I knew a Virginia years ago, she was a beautiful girl, in my 6th-grade class, who lived around the corner from me. Virginia's nickname was Ginny, and that suited this momma dog's personality! Besides it rhymed with skinny and boy was she! "Skinny Ginny" didn't actually stick. It just didn't feel right. But "Ginny'" was perfect.

As we reviewed the details of the rescue, we kept asking, both to ourselves and each other, "How could Wyatt possibly be alive?" His mother was starving. So emaciated that no one could believe she was alive let alone sustaining a puppy (or more) and giving birth! We didn't know if Wyatt was the only pup or the sole survivor. If there had been others, who did not make it, Ginny would have eaten them so that they would not attract predators. No one would blame her if she ate them to stay alive; it's what a desperate dog will do. It is more likely that Wyatt was an only pup. His mom was a young pit bull, and they often have single puppies, especially if it is their first litter. I would later check in with Charli, who assisted with the rescue and said Ginny never appeared pregnant. That told me Wyatt was, almost definitely, an only pup. If Ginny had been carrying a full litter, it would have been visible from a distance. I felt so much better knowing that was the case. I was also relieved that Ginny had such strong momma dog instincts that she cared for Wyatt like a pro! He was fat and healthy despite her near starvation. Certainly nursing him would have accelerated her weight loss as it takes a considerable calorie load to produce milk. Her production was pretty low but enough for one puppy!

Ginny and Wyatt were set up in my deluxe whelping kennel complete with whelping box, corrugated tin roof, shade cloth, igloo for chilly nights, blankets and a comforter. They would be very comfortable and protected from the weather and any predators that might like a puppy for dinner. We have coyotes, mountain lion, bear, eagles and owls, any of which would enjoy a plump puppy if they could get to him! Between the enclosed kennel and momma Ginny we were pretty sure Wyatt would be safe and warm. I started Ginny on a high calorie/high protein food but had to feed small amounts throughout the day. Reintroducing food too quickly can cause Refeeding Syndrome. RS results in fluid and electrolyte imbalances that can then cause fatal cardiac, pulmonary, or neurological episodes. We did know that a concerned person had started feeding her a few days before we got her and she had done well so, chances were that we were OK, but I wasn't taking any chances. We started with four feedings a day, and it was immediately a concern as she inhaled her food in just seconds. This meant we might face a second life-threatening feeding issue called Gastric Torsion or Bloat. Bloat is generally fatal. To slow Ginny down, I picked up a bowl specifically designed to slow the eating rate of dogs who wolf down their food. It was a perfect solution. Also, I started training her to "Wait" by holding a handful of food above her bowl. If she tried to get to it, I took it away. It didn't take long for her to catch on! In just days, she was waiting until I released the food into the bowl and gave her the "OKAY!"

Once Wyatt became mobile, (At just two and a half weeks! Most puppies don't really become mobile until about four weeks of age.) he was off and running. Fun to watch as his chubby legs were not yet strong enough to support the rest of his chubbiness! He'd climb the wall of the box, pulling himself up and over, and tumble to the ground. Determined little guy! He'd fall over repeatedly trying to get to his mother's food dish. He was too young to be introduced to solid food, and she wasn't going to share, but he tried. At first, Ginny was overly aggressive if he approached while she was eating. This caused some concern that she might really snap at him, and though plump, he was still tiny, and she could severely injure him. I didn't want her to hurt him defending dinner. That was the other motivation for the "Wait" exercise at feeding time; to calm Ginny down around food. The feeding by handfuls method helps a dog understand that there is always more coming. Starved dogs have experienced just the opposite, so they tend to guard food. Resource Guarding includes food and anything else a dog might consider of value - and it can be dangerous. I wanted to address that behavior ASAP.

Ginny was generally a non-aggressive girl, so I concluded these behaviors were more from circumstance than personality. With a little time, she would not feel so threatened, by a puppy or person near her food. By the time Wyatt was ready for his first mush, she not only was no longer defensive of her food, but she also left his alone until he was finished! I had some trepidation when I was introducing Wyatt to puppy food. I started by feeding mother and son in separate sections of the kennel so Ginny could not eat Wyatt's food nor snap if he approached. She really surprised me when I allowed them to first feed in the same area and she waited patiently for him to eat what he wanted. Again, her mothering instincts were perfect. I was moved to tears knowing how hungry she had been, and at that point still underweight by 10 pounds or more. It was only after Wyatt walked away from it, that she cleaned his little bowl. I praised her and gave her lots of love to let her know how good she was.

Part of what makes this story so emotional is how we were brought in on it. Ginny was in an area outside of Española that can be dangerous. Española is 25 minutes south of Dixon. Ginny was seen by some concerned neighbors. They talked to the owner, but he was confrontational and angry. Feeling that they hadn't made an impression, they called Animal Control to see if AC could help. The Animal Control Officer told them that they would go pick her up "next week." And that they had to "give the owner a chance." We all asked, "A chance for what? To kill her??!!" This was criminal animal abuse, and she was not going to live much longer without immediate intervention. Next week was far too late! What were they thinking?! Everyone involved with this rescue was shocked! Here, and in most jurisdictions, that kind of abuse and neglect is a felony. This conversation took place on a Thursday. The concerned neighbors decided that the answer they received from Animal Control was unacceptable and called the State Police Department. Animals are not part of the State Police's jurisdiction, but the neighbors were getting desperate for some help. This beautiful dog was going to die before anyone would help. A neighbor started to feed the dog so that she wouldn't starve to death but didn't feel that was enough to save this girl. They called their Veterinarian to ask what else they might be able to do. The Vet Clinic immediately called me. "Hey, Judy," I knew the voice on the other end, and the tone indicated there was an animal in need.

The caller filled me in on the situation and asked what we might be able to do. I had an empty kennel, but my schedule was full, so I was not available to go get the dog myself until Saturday. I asked for the address and realized I knew another rescuer that lived not far from there. I sent Katie a text that read, "Have you ever done a rogue rescue?" She said, "No, but I can do it! But not until Saturday morning." I called her to discuss the dangers of this rescue. No one wanted anyone to get hurt by the owner, who we believed could be dangerous. I told her to wait until I had more info. I could go down on Saturday with her to get the dog, safety in numbers, we hoped. It was the best we could do, and with the neighbors feeding the dog, she should be OK for the day. I received the contact info for the neighbors and while having a conversation about their experience with the owner and the dog she said the State Police had just called to inform her that the dog's owner was in jail. This was great news! It meant no one would be in danger. We could collect the dog and get her to the vet first thing Saturday morning and then foster her back to health. At least that was our plan.

Saturday morning, Katie called to see where we could meet on the highway to transfer the dog. She had gone in and found the mother dog to be very friendly until she approached the old dog house. As we chatted about the where and when she informed me that there was a puppy! Just one? We wondered if there had been others. When Katie went in to unchain the emaciated girl, she became very defensive near the dog house. That was the tip-off that there were pups. The mother dog was taken to the car for safety. With her confined to a crate in the car, into which she went very willingly, the pups could be brought out. It was remarkable that the momma was happy to be crated. This dog was so sweet and easy-going. The containment may have helped her to feel calm. Huge relief there! When Katie went back to the dog house, she only found the one pup. He was cold, so she popped him into her jacket to keep him warm and headed to the Vet Clinic.

The mother dog was covered in fleas and ticks, and I mean covered! Hundreds of them! None of us had ever seen such an infestation. I'm not squeamish, but my stomach did a somersault. It was just one more reason she should not have survived. Ticks also carry diseases that can kill a dog if untreated. She'd been living like this for some time. Thankfully the puppy was not covered as well. Momma was given an oral flea and tick treatment and a quick bath to kill many of the bugs instantly. Over the next couple of days, the rest would die and fall off. I pulled a few but was so grossed out I decided to let the medication do the job, I didn't have the stomach for it.

The meds did their job very quickly, and Ginny was tick-free in about three days. Though starved down to just skin and bones, Ginny was in relatively good health. The vet had run a blood panel to be sure she wasn't in organ failure or suffering from Heartworms. The tests were negative for both. How did she survive, let alone have a healthy pup? It defied reason, and yet, there she was. Katie, momma, and puppy met Mark and me at a local gas station to hand them off. As Katie pulled the tiny puppy from the warmth of her jacket, and handed him to me for the first time, it was then I lifted him up and named him Wyatt. By the time we transferred mother and pup to our car, Wyatt had been away from his mother for nearly four hours. He was only five days old and needed to nurse every couple of hours, so I put him in the crate with momma to nurse on our way home. She showed absolutely no aggression or fear as I opened the door and placed him under her. She didn't try to bolt or push past me to freedom. She just welcomed her puppy with a loving lick. She licked my hand as I released her beautiful boy to her care. I turned as the tears began. I thanked Katie for her help and promised regular updates. Mark and I headed back home to get this little family into their new home.

Over the next few weeks, we continued with some basic training. "Sit, down, wait, stay" commands as well as working on the jumping issue. Ginny was an enthusiastic jumper. Most dogs her age and breed are! If momma jumped to get her food, I turned away or started over if I had to. It didn't take long before she was sitting every time I approached the kennel. She sat and waited for her food. I would vary the delivery, hand fulls, pausing in between, a full bowl lowered to the ground very slowly or immediate delivery when she sat. Changing the delivery helps the learning process and quickly instills the desired behavior. She just kept proving what a smart girl she was. As Wyatt grew, he also exhibited some food aggression.

I worked with Wyatt while he ate by petting him and putting my hands in his bowl. Leaving your scent in the kibble helps them to recognize that hands are good! If he growled, I took the food away. He stopped growling after the second removal! Understand that I wouldn't use this method on a grown dog as I would probably get a bad bite, but since Wyatt was still a little pup, it was a safer bet. I knew he wasn't genuinely aggressive, just protecting his food. If I could teach him otherwise, that would be good for his future owner. Like his mother, he was a smart dog!

I had one of those moments tonight, the moments that leave me in awe of my canine companions and moved to tears by the depth of my love for these animals. It wasn't anything huge or particularly remarkable. It was a simple "sit" by eight-week-old Wyatt. Until just a few days ago Wyatt would jump up when I approached with his food. Ginny was "sitting" and "waiting" now instead of jumping and knocking her dish out of my hands. Her need to wolf down her food and then eat Wyatt's was causing Wyatt to eat far too fast.

I started by having Ginny "sit" and "wait" and then asking Wyatt to do the same. He had been hopping into his bed to eat there. It was so cute. But, he continued jumping for food. Not tonight! I said, "Wyatt, sit." And he did! It was so adorable and so brilliant of him. I had to laugh in awe of his intelligence and praise him before giving him dinner. In short order, this became his norm. When I approached the kennel, they would sit side by side, waiting for meals, treats, or just a visit. This was such a simple thing, and yet it felt so enormous. Neither of these beautiful creatures should have survived their neglect, however here they were and doing brilliantly! And I am so moved by them.

In October Wyatt went with me to Stray Hearts in Taos for his transfer to Colorado. Four other rescuers were dropping a truck-load of puppies, all a bit scared of what is happening and what comes next. They are kept separate since they have just started their puppy shots and don't have full immunity yet. We tried to reassure each puppy as they were loaded in.

During the loading process, I coaxed Wyatt out of the crate he rode in from my house to the Shelter. Wyatt was a bit nervous. He threw up during the ride, in the crate, good boy! Wyatt's only other car ride was at the age of five days when we rescued him. Once out of his crate, he crawled into my lap for comfort. I held him close as this was hard for me too. Our little miracle puppy was fat and healthy and ready for a new home. He wrapped his paws around my neck for one last hug. I was fighting back the tears as I got out of the car to put him in the travel kennel in the truck with the myriad of other puppies. He would travel alone in the crate. I so wished he had a littermate to keep him company but that wasn't to be.

As I approached the truck, everyone looked at us. A collective "Oh wow!" came from the group. Wyatt was three times the size of the other puppies. They ranged in age from six to 10 weeks. The Puppy Coordinator asked, "Five months?" "No, he's only 11 weeks," I replied. "He's a big boy!" She exclaimed. "Yup he sure is. And so sweet. I'm going to miss him." I choked before putting him in the truck. I told Wyatt it was going to be great! And that he should be a good boy for his new family as I wiped at my tears. It is always hard to say goodbye. This one even more so because he was an only pup. A litter becomes overwhelming to care for by this age. They have each other to bond and play with, so there is less of a connection to me. Wyatt only had his mom and me. Both bonds were strong. This was the first time he'd been away from Ginny, and now I was leaving him too.

The 24th of October was a Wednesday. The next adoption event at Colorado Puppy Rescue was Saturday the 27th. All of the puppies we sent were up for adoption, and all of them found homes that day! Often the puppies are not adopted immediately. If they have a large group of pups and fewer adopters, it may take two or three events before they find homes. I checked the Puppy Rescue website daily at first, then every few days, then once a week until finally the adoption photos were posted. Usually, they post soon after an event, but this time it took weeks! It was so hard waiting to see who fell in love with him. I remember my first transfer puppy, Sienna. She was a beautiful red-brown Heeler mix. Gorgeous pup, sweet, super smart, good with other dogs, just a great puppy. I had thought about keeping her, but I was still settling in after my divorce and just didn't want another dog. I regretted sending her away as soon as I did it, but I thought some beautiful family, perhaps one that lived on a farm where she could run, would take her home. I waited anxiously for those adoption photos to post. She was adopted and their beaming faces and the love in their eyes showed that they adored this girl. She had found her home.

I had a little break recently for the Holidays and to ski with Mark's boys in Colorado. I couldn't have children and have envied my friends becoming grandparents in the past few years. Mark's boys and their wives each had their first child this past year, so we had baby time in Colorado too. Bright, happy babies! One boy and one girl. But all that fun left me too tired to write and to some degree without inspiration. Work with Ginny had come to a standstill. Buddy, the neighbor's dog comes over every day, and Ginny just gets crazy excited. I watched for signs of aggression but didn't generally see any. When she gets that worked up, I cannot get through to her. It's as if I'm not there. I was getting discouraged and concerned that Ginny wasn't doing well being so isolated. I felt I was failing her.

A local friend had a Christmas open house, and since we weren't leaving until the Thursday after Christmas, we went. Since the crowds were departing, it gave us some excellent chat time. We talked dog! Our hosts were dog rescuers as well and had a pit mix who was a challenging case, but with time, she had settled down and became a lovely dog. I opened the possibility of them taking Ginny when the time came. That was not exactly embraced. I can't say I didn't try. The son had dog training experience, so I asked if he might be willing to work with Ginny once a week on harness as I was concerned that she would pull me off my feet if I attempted to walk her. My request was met with silence. I really couldn't wait for him to come on board. Ginny needed to get out.

I was out working with Ginny on harness in the kennel. Mostly I wanted to get her used to wearing it, in preparation for a walk. She didn't seem to mind it at all but getting her to sit still long enough to put it on was a challenge! She was just so excitable and always on the lookout for Buddy. When Buddy arrived, she'd bark excitedly, running back and forth in the kennel. At her previous residence, she was tied out 24/7. Neither human nor dog interaction. Other neighborhood dogs may have wandered over, but it is pretty clear that Ginny had never been socialized.

Buddy might be the perfect dog to help with that if Ginny isn't too aggressive. Mark was away for a few days, so not the day to introduce them. I needed backup. I was desperate to make some sort of progress with her, though. I needed it, and she certainly needed it. It just isn't fair to keep her kenneled alone all the time. She needed to get out on daily walks and learn to be a real dog! The holidays were always hectic, and then there was snow, lots of snow. A foot of snow made the dog walks a real challenge. Beyond wading through it, it gets very slippery both in my driveway and on the road. With a trained dog like Josie, it wasn't so bad, but I wasn't willing to take the risk with an untrained dog that was going to be a champion puller.

Ginny stayed in her kennel, barking at Buddy, and we did training sessions on her other commands. She was great at sit, wait, down, and come as long as Buddy was nowhere in sight. When he showed, Ginny started her barking frenzy, and it was time for me to do something else. I often wondered what she would do if given a chance to meet Buddy face to face.

One morning, I managed to get the harness on in reasonably short order and worked on sit, wait, down and walked around the kennel keeping her focused. Just being together, working together, was important too. She seemed pretty comfortable, but the enclosure is just not big enough to get a real sense of walking on a leash. Buddy had not made his way over yet, so I thought, "Why not?" "Why not take her out of the kennel and see how she is?" Before I did that, I went to find a second leash so that I could have one on her harness and one on her collar just in case Buddy showed, and we had a problem. Ginny has a harness that hangs from the kennel door along with her leash. It is an excellent harness and strong leash, but she is so powerful I just didn't trust it to hold if she really pulled. She is not a large dog at 55 pounds, but she is well muscled! I added the second leash and out we went. She did not bolt as anticipated, she just wanted to explore. And she pulled, but I can pull harder. This was actually very good to know! I was concerned that she would be so strong that I had no hope of controlling her if she showed aggression. If she was pumped with adrenalin, she might still win, but so far, I was able to hold her back with one arm. As soon as the little dogs out in their yard saw her, they started their yapping chorus. So tough those little ones! Ginny immediately headed toward the Littles' outdoor pen. She didn't tug or pull. She approached fairly calmly. The Littles started yapping again as she got close, louder this time, and snapping, mostly at each other. Ginny just stood there looking at them. She seemed curious, but she showed absolutely no inclination to even bark back! They came nose to nose through the fence. She extended her nose and gave a sniff, but she did not react to their noise at all! I told the Littles that they had made enough noise thank you, and we started to explore the snow in the side yard. This may have been Ginny's only experience with snow. She liked it. We suspect Wyatt was her first pregnancy at about six months old, probably on her first heat cycle. That puts Ginny at just over a year old now. We didn't have much snow last winter so it may well be the first she has seen. She romped in it a bit and suddenly turned. "Uh, oh," I thought. "Here we go! " as I turned to see what had caught her attention. Sure enough, Buddy had arrived. I prepared for the worst by taking the leashes in both hands and edging toward the kennel. I had to be ready to pull her away if she attacked. To my surprise and delight, she approached Buddy calmly, at least as calmly as Ginny can! Buddy is so non-reactive I held out hope that this would be OK. And it was! Buddy stood still as Ginny approached. She walked right over and stuck her nose in his rear. OK! Hello Buddy! "Now, what will she do?" I wondered if she'd show dominance or test him with a bark. But SHE TURNED AWAY!

I was amazed!! She seemed completely disinterested! This is the dog she goes crazy over every time he visits. Disinterested? What?! Incredible. Then she turned back. Now she was showing a bit of dominance, and since I was alone, I cut the visit short. I gave her a tug and a command to go in her kennel. She did so without much hesitation and no fight. I was so excited I had to text Jeannie and Mark. This was big! It looked like Ginny and Buddy would be friends in short order. This dog is so amazing. She just needs the opportunity to become. Become whole and loved and learn a different kind of life than what she has known. This inspires me! I am so grateful to these dogs to have the chance to show them that people are not all mean, abusive, or negligent. I have the honor to teach them how to trust again or possibly for the first time. Yes, this inspires me.

Since the meet and greet went so well, Mark and I took her out for a full-on introduction. Sniffing, growling, mounting, whatever they needed to do to determine who is the boss. Dogs always have a hierarchy. The Alpha will establish dominance in short order by mounting or taking a mouthful of scruff, or with a full out fight. Buddy has always been so submissive that we didn't think a battle would ensue, but I wasn't yet sure of Ginny's temperament around other dogs. She didn't seem to be an Alpha, but she had been rough enough with Wyatt to give me a bit of concern. We would just proceed with caution. Mark grabbed one leash, and I grabbed the other as we exited the kennel in case we had to pull Ginny off of Buddy. Buddy was already in the yard, and as we approached, he kept his distance. Not a good sign. It meant he was cautious too. I asked Mark to keep moving toward him slowly, which was difficult as Ginny was pulling like crazy! Understand Mark is a six and a half foot tall athlete so no weakling! And I was helping hold her back as well.

We needed to know if they would get along, so we proceeded, ready to pull back at any second but trying very hard not to give any negative vibe. If we were afraid the dogs would pick up on it and could feed any aggression. Buddy decided it was OK to approach. We watched intently as they did exactly what they did the other day. Butt sniff and disinterest! They went nose to nose, nose to rear, and back a couple of times and we stopped holding Ginny back. It was abundantly clear that she was non-aggressive. At least with Buddy! Time to go for a walk!!

Ginny is a champion puller, even on a harness. To curb this, I use two methods. One is to stop. Yup, that simple. At the Humane Society, we called this "tree." Each time a dog pulls you stand unmoving, like a tree. Super simple, not always easy if you have a champion puller, but doable. And the harness helps. It has a front hook so that when the dog pulls, and the walker pulls back, it refocuses the dog's attention back to the walker. Some dogs will learn very quickly that if they don't want to be stopping all the time, then they have to stop pulling. Others, well it takes a little patience!

Since I had a coupon to the pet store, I stopped in the next day in Santa Fe and found a nice heavy, padded harness that looked like it might do the job. I admit it still surprises me that she will just stand and allow me to harness her. Even when Buddy is near, and she is doing her crazy dog dance for him! We have continued with the daily walks with Buddy.

It had just started to flurry as we headed out. I'd decided to take Ginny first as she is the stronger of the two so it takes more from me if she decides to pull. She put her harness on as always, no big deal. She sat at each kennel door (there are two), waited as commanded until I opened the door. When I released her with an "OK!" she went bonkers, nuts, boffo, for the snow. Totally bat poop crazy! Josie loves the snow too, but she is half husky - it makes sense! This is a short-coated pibble, she should hate it, but she doesn't. We had had snow previously and since it warms during the day and refreezes at night the driveway was covered in ice and compacted snow. With the new snow on the old snow and ice, it was pretty slippery. Ginny didn't care and started to pull and pull hard! I stood my ground, being a tree. I so wished I could just let her off to run wildly through the falling snow, but I didn't dare. I wasn't sure she would come back if she bolted. She and Buddy are beautiful together, but some of the other neighborhood dogs might not be so friendly. The last thing I wanted was a dog fight. Visions of Blondie's death just wouldn't allow me to give her that kind of freedom. So I held on. She did eventually calm, and we headed up the driveway. The flurries now done, it was a full-on blizzard! And Ginny went nuts again. Jumping and pulling and I don't even know what she wanted to do, perhaps just run in it, but I couldn't let her run free. We walked about a quarter-mile, and she was not following voice commands, the road was getting dangerously slick, and she was pulling harder than ever. I was imagining being dragged for miles through piling snow and decided to go home. The pulling contest on the slippery road left me tired, sweaty, and discouraged. Had I failed? Was she going to pull like this from now on? Or was it just the snow was so exciting she couldn't contain herself? I so hoped it was the latter. She went back into her kennel without much fuss.

I grabbed a drink of water and went in to get Josie. I so hoped she wasn't as excited as Ginny about the now two inches of snow that had fallen in the past 30 minutes. It was still coming down so heavily I couldn't see through my glasses! I went in and harnessed Josie expecting a full repeat of the experience with Ginny. I didn't have it in me to do again so if she was crazy in the snow we were not going to walk this morning, no way. Josie was better. She loved snow, but she wanted to roll in it and eat as much as she could, everywhere! She too was pulling more than usual but not like Ginny. We went on a regular length walk, stopped for a few pictures, and headed back. By the time we reached the house, I was soaked to the skin and ready for a hot shower. Glad they had both gotten their walks, but I was spent.

It was now mid-February; we woke to a world blanketed in the fluffiest powder snow I'd seen in a long time. I love the quiet of a good snowfall. It was still coming down, so I decided to wait and see if it was going to let up or not. The snow was forecast for the rest of the day, but it looked like a midday break was coming. I harnessed Ginny and prepared myself for more out of control behavior once we left the kennel. Buddy, as always now, was there to go with us. He shows up for almost every walk. How does Buddy know?! He stood just a few feet from the kennel patiently awaiting the greeting Ginny would bring. He had been joining in just about every day, and he and Ginny had become good friends. Ginny's greeting was more of a full-on attack, but Buddy had learned that it was just play, and greeted her with equal enthusiasm.

In the early days, he was a bit taken aback by her aggressiveness; now that he understood her better, they were so fun to watch! They'd jump and roll, a growl here and there from Buddy, to say "go easy" and they are done. At least for the moment, and we head out. Again we had snow on ice, so it was slippery in places, but Ginny was so much better at not pulling that it was a pleasure to walk in the fresh whiteness that surrounded us. At least until it was time to go back to the kennel. Mark had come out to walk with us, and that set Ginny off, pulling and lunging. She really just wanted to greet him in much the same way she greets Buddy, but that is not acceptable behavior! I stood my ground and held against her pulling once again with sweat running down my neck. This is one tenacious dog! I held her until Mark approached and ignored her jumping, but she was not going to relent. He went back to the house while I kenneled Ginny. Once Mark was out of view, she calmed, entered the kennel, and waited calmly while I unharnessed her. When she is quiet like that, I get a picture of how she will be with a little more time and training. I remind myself of where Ginny was not too many months ago and how far this girl has come in a relatively short time. She truly inspires me both to share her story and to continue my work with her. In the beginning, I just wasn't sure how Ginny would do. Even with daily training, I wasn't convinced that she would heal from the abuse and neglect she suffered for that first year of her short life. But she is resilient, most dogs are. Far more than we humans. So we will continue this work and hope to find Ginny a perfect forever home in the not too distant future. She may end up as a permanent resident with me. In that case, she will be introduced to the Littles and get to be an indoor dog. For me, not ideal, but we will do what she needs to feel safe and loved. Being part of my pack might be just what she needs.

It has been a few weeks, Ginny is still here though she has been posted in a couple of places on-line as available for adoption. As time goes on, she is calming down and is a joy to work with. Of course, that makes it harder to let her go. The more I know her, the more I adore her! While we were out today before a major storm hit, I was thinking about coming back to continue with the Tui story. I was struck by the fact that it was exactly three years ago. Time is getting stranger, I swear. It seems both like just yesterday and so long ago that I rescued Tui and watched her whelp her pups. And what a beautiful end to her story. I so hope Ginny will find a similar adopter.

Jeannie and I were talking about a small dog that was attacked, and due to past history, the Vet would not take the case. This is becoming more common as our local Vets are getting stiffed on bills. It is causing them to turn animals away. We help when we can, but we can't cover every incident. Jeannie was telling me that one of the Vets suggested she write a book of her stories, she has 30 years worth! She said, "No way! I don't want to relive them all." Oh, I so get that! Almost every story in this book has a positive ending, but there are many over the years that do not. I can tell you that reliving these has been difficult enough. While I'm in the middle of a rescue, it doesn't seem that hard. I suppose because we just do what needs to be done at the moment, but given some hindsight, it's different. For now, I'm loving the Ginny story and watching her become a sweet, confident dog.

Animal Rescue Explained
by Ashley Owen Hill

The neglect changes you.
The abuse hardens you.
The suffering breaks you.
The ignorance angers you.
The indifference disturbs you.
The injustice destroys you.

On a daily basis…your faith will be tested.
Your heart will be wounded….
Your soul will be altered.

On a weekly basis…you'll question yourself.
You'll question your strength.
You'll question the world.

On a monthly basis…you'll fall down.
You'll get up.
You'll go on…

On a yearly basis…you'll look back…
You'll see faces…
You couldn't save them.
You'll learn to mourn.
To grieve.
To sob.
You'll learn to trust a little less.
To do a little more.
To fight a little harder.
You'll learn to try.
To hope.

To pray.
You'll learn to fail.
To succeed.
To accept.
You'll learn when to hold on.
When to give up.
When to let go.
You'll learn who you are.
What you stand for.
Why that matters.

Then… at times… you'll forget why you matter.
You'll question what you're doing.
You'll wonder if it's worth it.

But…here's the good news… When you forget…
When you question…
When you wonder…
All you have to do…
Is take a look around…
And you'll see them.

You'll see their faces.
You'll see their smiles.
You'll feel their love.

In their eyes, you'll see their journeys…
You'll remember their beginnings…
You'll know how far they've come…
You'll remember when they didn't know you…
When they didn't trust you…
When they'd given up.

You'll remember how you healed them…
How you loved them…
How they loved you, too.
And as you look back…
You'll want to move forward…
For them… and because of them.

In your darkest hours, you'll look around…
To find the differences made…the hope given…and the
lives saved…
Because you existed.
In those moments, when you look into their eyes…every
doubt will be erased.
Every question will be answered.
Every worry will subside.
Because in that instant…in each of your hearts…
You both share the very same thought: "Every bit of pain
was worth it…for this moment here with you."
And honestly…no matter what else happens…
Those moments hold all the strength you need…
To keep going.

Rescue is pain.
Rescue is joy.
Rescue is worth it…because they are worth it.
And that's the honest truth.

Conclusion

Where there is Sunshine there is deep shadow

When I started the book, I spoke with my friend Pat, with whom I had worked, years ago, at the Agency in Providence. Pat was the CD/Copy to my CD/Art. And, she was like a big sister to me. Pat died this past spring, and I miss her dearly. She was to be my editor. (I am forever indebted to Adele who stepped into the editor job. I could not have finished this without her invaluable input!) I spoke with Pat every few months to catch up on life. During a drive to Santa Fe, she told me, "Keep writing, and a thread will appear." I had started to compose the stories but was as yet unsure where it was going. I insisted it was just a collection of rescue stories. On my way home later that day, I had to pull over to call her back when it hit me like a ton of bricks. Sunshine was my fist rescue here and the first to reveal shadows I had not previously seen. I can't say if they were not evident or if I was just not aware but, ultimately it doesn't matter. They were visible to me now. With each rescue I became more aware.

I did not want the book to be about the issues in the marriage/relationships. I did want it to be about my awakening and coming into my personal power to do something about it. I have tried to keep the issues as an undercurrent with just enough revealed to allow a sense of the difficulties and my struggle with them.

With each issue I wrestled with the questions I was asked to ask of myself. "Can I live with it?" *and* "Is it enough?" At times the answers were yes, or yes, for now. But, as time went on the yeses were fewer and the nos more numerous and louder. When I witnessed the physical force against an abused pup that was more than I could tolerate. I knew then that I had to leave the marriage.

Once I left the marriage (I was devastated, it was the last thing I wanted but the only option I had left. When I left Providence to live with my husband in Texas I said goodbye to my family and friends, my studio and students, and my sources of income. The move to NM further reduced my options for generating an income. At the time that was fine, we were moving to live a slower life, get out of the rat race that was central Texas. But after the divorce there were far fewer skaters so the Skate Shop would not generate enough to support myself. The guest house at the home we built would generate a nice income but I wouldn't be living there. Selling my art work wasn't paying off; I had no idea what I was going to do!) I was in a fog; six weeks of packing while desperately searching for a place to live. With the rescue dogs, I couldn't rent. With the minimal settlement I would receive, my options for buying -property is very expensive here - were limited. And yet, a nearly perfect solution presented itself! Jeannie pushed me to buy it, I had no alternative, I had to!

I saw that I needed to have faith. That is something I have struggled with mightily. I have not felt like the Universe has my back. If anything I've felt the opposite, but I was learning, opening, awakening. I love where I live now. The night skies are breathtaking. The neighbors are good people. It is quiet. I don't think we realize the level of noise we are subjected to until we go somewhere quiet. At night the bats fly close without a sound; the mournful coyote chirps and howls echo through the hills. A faint rustle of leaves on a breeze. Owls hoo hoo, both beautiful and haunting. But no traffic, few sirens, no raised voices or loud music save the occasional party. Peace. I found a peaceful place to heal and rebuild.

One afternoon, while talking to a friend about the end of the marriage, she shared this poem:

One day you finally knew
what you had to do, and began,
though the voices around you
kept shouting

their bad advice --
though the whole house
began to tremble
and you felt the old tug
at your ankles.
"Mend my life!"
each voice cried.
But you didn't stop.
You knew what you had to do,
though the wind pried
with its stiff fingers
at the very foundations,
though their melancholy
was terrible.
It was already late
enough, and a wild night,
and the road full of fallen
branches and stones.
But little by little,
as you left their voice behind,
the stars began to burn
through the sheets of clouds,
and there was a new voice
which you slowly
recognized as your own,
that kept you company
as you strode deeper and deeper
into the world,
determined to do
the only thing you could do --
determined to save
the only life that you could save.

Mary Oliver - *The Journey*

So, with little financial support and no way to make a living due to the CFS, what was I to do? I did all I could do, putting one foot in front of the other. I went back to teaching skating; it has been a passion since childhood. Teaching feeds my soul. Sharing my love and knowledge of the sport with others young and old inspires me. It would also bring in a little bit of income. I can only make the rink twice a week, or I am too tired to move. So I strike a balance of work/rest and hope it keeps working. In between I have the rescue work. It does not bring in any income, but it offers grounding and connection. But I kept questioning myself, how can I possibly stay with it? Should I be doing something else? Each time I asked this, sometimes even out loud, another rescue would be upon me!

Another rescue was always right there to provide me with focus and remind me, once again, that I was needed, here, now. That intense focus on the wellbeing of another took me out of my head and back into my heart. The soul connection was so healing. The dogs and cats give love so freely; all they ask in return is a bowl of kibble and a pat on the head, a belly rub, or to sit in your lap. Or, my favorite, puppy kisses. So simple. So pure.

With each rescue, it became more evident that *THIS* is exactly what I "should" be doing. It is my calling; I can no longer ignore the call. I am continually receiving little reminders, like yesterday. A couple of Dixon kids, now in their 20s, were married at home on the farm. I stopped in after teaching to dance and celebrate with these incredible young people. As soon as I came through the gate, the resident dog, generally aloof and timid, came right over to me for comfort. The crowd and the loud music were clearly a challenge for her, and she was seeking a connection. She pressed up against me, and I sat so she could place her head in my lap. Was I the only one she was going to? You bet! I watched as she wandered through the crowd, but she didn't stop to check in with anyone else. Not even her owner. Would others have noticed? Probably not. These are the moments that fill my heart and let me know to keep going.

Tui was one of the dogs that arrived as I was experiencing a dark night of the soul. I'd broken up with the man I was seeing after he told me he couldn't trust me. He reassured me I'd done nothing to make him think he couldn't trust me, but he couldn't. (I know, it didn't make any sense to me either.) I took it as a projection and a clear indication that a relationship with him would not work. So, there I was alone again. (That was very difficult for me at the time, not so difficult now.) and, as I often did, started to question what I was doing with my life, how I would support myself when my funds ran out, etc.? Yes, tedious. This was a thought process that could spin down into the darkness in no time! I was back to the "should I?" question of being in rescue. Like the medicine wheel, I appeared to be in the same place *again*. But it really was never the same place twice was it? Each time I experienced one of these dark times, I learned something about myself, what I wanted or didn't want in a relationship, even questioning if I want to be in a relationship *at all*. For me this was a revelation! I grew up believing I would marry and stay married to one man. And, a woman wasn't complete without a man. That's what our parents did - right?! It's what we were taught was right. So as I grew, my perspective changed, albeit sometimes only a micron, but it was different each time.

Being a CFS sufferer, the emotional and energetic toll of a breakup was huge. It always sent me into a deep and exhausted state for a while. (This too is easier now than it was four or five years ago.) Blondie, Momma B, Aurora, Tui, and others, came right at a time that I needed a reminder that I was doing *EXACTLY* what I "*Should*" be doing! My connection to the animals was so deep and so healing to both them and me, that I really couldn't deny it any longer. And really *should* have stopped questioning it but sometimes we need to revisit something, repeatedly, for it to really sink in. I was in a place where I knew it but was not quite ready to truly embrace it. And what was that? Why did I need to question? (This wasn't going to be the last time.) I could hear the voices in my head telling me I was wasting an education. That I "should" go back into design or advertising. I'd done that and knew it would once again eat away at my soul. Full-time employment isn't possible; the stress of a typical work environment would land me in deep trouble very quickly. I wasn't willing to test it. The thought of being hospitalized and bedridden was enough to halt that train of thought. The price was just too high. So, I would just have to figure out how to continue my work and make a living.

Aurora, Danaka, Blondie, Tui, Dottie, Josie (those last three in close succession) and Ginny. In between, there were feral cats like Momma B., where my involvement was fairly minimal. (Momma B. had a litter in my care.) Each had lessons for me. In some cases, I was dating, and a rescue revealed an issue I could not continue in a relationship with. A trust issue. Issues with intimacy. So hard under the best of circumstances, but without the shared skills to work through them, we'd just end up circling the same issue with no healing, no resolution, and no intimacy. Narcissism, with no empathy. Some complained about the animals and wanted me to get rid of them. With the end of each relationship, I grew. Learning what I would not accept any more. So much of me had been sacrificed for the good of relationship. There is always compromise, but there needs to be balance, and I wasn't finding it. For now, I was the one who could give me what I was seeking. I could love me and the animals could too. My circle of friends give me the support I need. I could live with that, and yes, it was enough.

I have had the conversation, about choosing not to be in relationship, with a number of single female friends and they all have had similar experiences. We are choosing to live our lives in a way that nurtures and honors *us*. (Some of my married/partnered friends are envious.) As women, for so long we have subjugated our own needs or wants for the good of the relationship and we just aren't doing that anymore. We want our lives to have meaning; *on our terms*. Would we like to be in relationship? Perhaps, but not if it requires the sacrifices we've made in the past. We hear that the Patriarchy has crumbled but it will take time for the dust to settle and a new way of being to emerge. Until then we gather to talk, encourage, care for each other, and muddle through. I don't want you to get the wrong impression, it isn't easy, but we value our independence as we continue to grow as women and human beings.

An old friend from childhood asked me the other day if I'd ever remarry. He is a very kind man, whose wife is also in animal rescue, so he understands my world pretty well. I told him I couldn't answer that, but at the present moment it was unlikely. I have no way of knowing what lies ahead. I will keep my heart open to possibilities, as they are numerous and as yet unseen. For now I live my life on my terms and I am finding that to be very fulfilling. Admittedly, much to my surprise!

I feel like I finally own this gift of animal connection. More than ever, my community is acknowledging my work and the difference it is making. I guess that's why I felt compelled to write this book. Not that I really had a choice! At one point I felt a physical shove to write. A literal push, as if someone was there behind me. It consumed me. I talked to everyone about it, then Ondrea showed me how to begin. It was time to share this with anyone interested on any level. My work doesn't change the world, but it changes my world and the animals' who share it.

Three days ago a litter of semi-feral kittens was dumped at the Post Office. One of them, the smallest, has a broken back so he cannot walk. I have named him Tiny Tim. At the Library on Saturdays we have a STEM (Science, Technology, Engineering and Math) workshop for the kids. Right now one of the leaders is working on 3-D printed human prosthetics so we are going to have the kids design and print a wheelchair for Tiny Tim! Oh, I so love what I do!

Pablo Picasso is quoted as saying,

"The meaning of life is to find your gift. The purpose of life is to share it."

I encourage everyone to find what feeds their soul, find *your* passion and live it. Life is pretty empty without it. Don't let anyone else tell you what you "should" or shouldn't be doing! It is your life, live it for you! I may not make a lot of money or live in a big beautiful house, but my life is full and beautiful. My heart sings every day, living and working with the rescue critters.

I am also blessed to have such dedicated, talented skating students who inspire me to be a better coach each time I work with them. None of them will be Olympians but each is growing in their skills and confidence and that carries out into the world. My student that is a high school senior is going to study Political Science. I can't wait to see how she helps shape a better world. Right now we are putting together our numbers for the annual Holiday Ice Show. Each is pushing beyond their comfort zone to grow as a skater and performer. Nothing could be better! We can and must all live lives of passion, we just need to listen to what awakens us. Stop putting it off. It will change you, empower you, ground you and make you feel more you than ever before. And that is your purpose here, now. To find you soul work and do it.

Thank you for taking the time to read these stories; I do hope they give you the inspiration to find your meaning and purpose, then share it. Writing this book changed me in ways I can't even put into words, yet. I learned more compassion for my fellow humans, deeper knowing that what I do is what I need to do. Who I am is who I need to be. For me, and the animals in my world. You don't need to write a book about your passion or soul work, but find a way that works for you, to share.

And support your local rescues; we need you.

Photo of the Author and Baby Girl, another rescue, by Mark Massey

I'll leave you with this excerpt from a poem I found when I had just started the book. I already had decided on the title, so I acknowledged this as another nudge from the universe that it was time to write it. It so beautifully describes my experience.

Dog Days of Summer - Meena Alexander

In the dog days of summer as muslin curls on its own heat
And crickets cry in the black walnut tree

The wind lifts up my life
And sets it some distance from where it was......

Appendix

This is a diary of training with Josie. She has some deep fears, particularly of vehicles, and it has taken time and patience to overcome.

Update April 5, 2018

Three days ago was the first time I was able to get Josie in a vehicle! For the past few months, we have gone for a walk nearly every day. We work on sit, down, stay, and steady a.k.a heel. When we return home I sit in my old RAV4, a vehicle I purchased because my car is frighteningly bad in the snow. I share the RAV with the rescue as our old Ford Pickup is just-that-old. The RAV is better in many situations such as off-road rescues. Anyway, I sit in the driver's seat and offer Josie high value treats like hot dogs, Mark's (my current partner) leftover beef or pork, or other yummy (to a dog) treats. For weeks now she would put her paws on my leg but would come no further. I started to leave the door open on the passenger side and slide into the driver's seat in hopes that she would climb up to get treats on my side. High expectations! She wouldn't do it. She would put her front paws on the floor and reach halfway across the seat but refused to come in any farther. I started to call this "Go for a ride" in my crazy dog lady voice all excited and sounded like I was on something. I was beginning to think it would be easier if I were! On Monday we did our usual walk and came back to the car, but this time when I said "Come up" and patted her seat - she jumped in!! I showered her with praise and kisses and all the treats I had in my training pouch! I was sure this was a fluke, that she would not do it ever again. On Tuesday, we did the usual routine in the morning. Walk and "Go for a ride." To my amazement, she jumped in! More praise more treats and more crazy dog lady voice. Had we turned a corner? Just to see I went out late Tuesday afternoon to do it again. Would she? I went to the studio kennel as always, opened the door and called "Walkies!" and she ran the other way. This dog is so smart she recognized a change in our routine and wondered what I was up to! Holy brilliance! I called her over and treated her, but she refused to let me put her walking harness on. She didn't count on my stubbornness. I often tell dogs I will out-stubborn them so they might as well give in. I didn't tell Josie this; I gave her space. This was not the time to out-stubborn anyone. I did not want to lose the headway I had gained. After a couple of minutes, she came right over and sat for her harness. Still wary of what was up though. We went for our walk and then came back to the car. She hesitated, but only for a second. I opened the car door, and she followed me right in! Praise, treats, tears flowed freely. Yes, we had turned a corner, broken through her abject fear of a vehicle; I was elated!

For the past year, I have allowed Josie to run in the evening to burn off some energy, have some freedom like she used to, and just enjoy her time out of the kennel. About 6 months ago she returned with a gaping gash under her right front leg. Apparently, she did not clear the barbed wire that is in a few places along the fence. This was a significant problem since I could not get her to the vet for suturing. Dr. Kim came over to have a look at it. She instructed me to clean the wound and start her on antibiotics, and with time, it would heal completely. It did, but it took weeks. Had it been sutured it would have improved in days. That was the last free night run for Josie. With mountain lion and bobcat spotted in the area, there were too many risks. She needed to get out regularly, so we started walking and training again. I admit I had pretty much given up on her as anything more than a kennel dog. Now that she was a little older and has spent time with the other dogs, she does seem to be settling in and becoming more responsive to training. At this very moment, she is licking the bone on the back seat! Finally, comfortable enough in the car to relax and at least taste the bone. Baby steps but progress! ! I adore this dog. She is so smart and so beautiful. She has suffered abuses we can only guess at. Even if I get her to enjoy the car, going for rides and deem her adoptable, I may not be able to part with her. This is the rub. The tough ones who require so much from us are the ones with whom we bond so profoundly.

It is now Friday, April 6, Josie an I are in the RAV, doors closed, just hanging out while I write. She is nervous, not really enjoying the bone. It's a marrow bone from the meat market, which every dog I've ever known has grabbed and defended to the death. Your death, of course, or that of the bone. But her not just devouring it tells me she is nervous. (Later I will give it to her in the kennel, and she will grab it and run! No way will she let the other dogs anywhere near her bone.)

She has just climbed into the back seat all on her own!! That's another first! I moved the bone to the back and will see if she calms enough to enjoy it. After writing for a little bit, I glanced back, and yes, she is licking the bone! I tried not to be seen, but she is so tuned in there was no way I could check without her knowing. Checking on her raises her suspicion, so I don't want to keep putting her on alert. In the next couple of weeks, I will continue this desensitization and eventually will start the car. I suspect that will be an issue, but we'll see!

April 11 update.

We have been in the car everyday but for shorter periods as it has been warm lately. At first, she is reluctant to even get in the car but then decides it is OK. It seems it has to be her decision, ultimately. She will only get in through the passenger front seat so far. This means I have to get in first and climb over the stick to the driver's seat. Another time that it is good that I'm small and flexible or that just wouldn't work! Unfortunately, the back doors do not stay open on their own, which scares her, or I think she would get in from there. Perhaps in due time. Once she is in, she still shows signs of nervousness; glancing around, panting, not sitting still. After a bowl of water and some treats she is settling, some. Twice I have turned on the electrical, so I could lower the windows and just that, with the sound of the radio, the vent fan and the windows, makes her jumpy. But just nervous, not a full-blown panic. This is actually a significant intermediate step to work up to starting the car. I'll continue with it for a bit until it no longer elicits the fear response. And that may be a while.

May 2

We sat in the car for an hour today, windows moving up and down; the radio off and on. Josie still reacts to the windows moving but less than she did. I was on the phone dealing with Wolf hybrids running loose and a horse with a pastern infection possibly from barbed wire, so not paying much attention to Josie. She did settle and lie down on the back seat. But she has yet to dive into her marrow bone with any enthusiasm. When she does, I will take that as a sign that she is comfortable in the car. Until then, I will not start the engine. I know how she is!

We have now been working on "down" for a few weeks, during our walks. Josie learned the hand signal very quickly, nothing new there! I introduced the voice command and used both for a while then tried just voice command - nothing. For two weeks, she completely ignored the voice command. I went back to the hand signal with voice command and had a 100% response. Then I moved to a partial hand signal (the full sign is hand in a fist at my waist lowered to the ground. With a partial the fist is only moved downward slightly) and voice command. As soon as my hand started moving down, so did she! Then if I just bent over, down, she went. Now all I have to do it think about the voice command and down she goes! Like she can read my mind. We are adding "Stay" to her repertoire as well. No long term stays yet, but she has the idea. Her stubborn streak may make that one a challenge. We'll see!

May 19

It is with a bursting heart that I attempt to write this through overflowing tears of joy! A couple of days ago, I started the RAV4 and left it running as I went to the Studio kennel to harness Josie for our training session. The RAV isn't far from the Studio so Josie could hear it running. There was no way I was getting the harness on her with the car running. The fear on her face was evident. She wasn't letting me anywhere near! After turning the engine off, I returned to harness her and go on our walk. At first hesitant and unwilling to "come," I gave her a moment, and she was ready. Harnessed and prepared to walk, we headed out. She darted away from the car, obviously still very fearful. Our walk was the usual practicing "sit," "down," "stay," as always. When we returned, instead of heading to the kennel, I walked Josie to the car. She followed right along and hopped in without hesitation. This was a relief as I had some concern that the fear would linger. I was extremely cautious with the training, cognizant that any fright could set us back weeks if not months. But she seemed to recover quickly that morning. Today, I once again started the RAV4 and left it running. Still, Josie was hesitant to don her harness but not as frightened as previously. She usually meets me in the hallway to put it on, today I had to harness her in the kennel, but she sat patiently while I clipped her in.

Josie did give me one little whine as I buckled the harness. She used to whine in fear as she was harnessed but hasn't for some time. I thanked her for allowing me to harness her, and we headed out. This time she did not bolt away from the car! OK! I turned toward the RAV, and she followed right along, wow! Would she balk as I asked her to get in? No! She followed me right in! "Josie you are amazing!" I told her. I showered her with love and treats! She looked at the front of the car and listened to the engine.

I assumed she was determining if it was something of which to be afraid. She then turned and licked my face. This assures me that she is comfortable. Not yet excited to "go for a ride." But feels safe in a running car. I turned the car off and watched her cock her head listening. I asked her, "Should I start it again?" She slurped my face! I took that as a yes and started it up. She didn't even flinch! ! She continued to listen and look at the dash and the hood. As I turned it off, she was curious about the key. What I wouldn't give to know what she was thinking! I was thinking, "This is huge!" More praise and treats for Josie and we'll do it again and again until I see that she is calm enough that I dare to put it into gear. I tell her she'll love going for a ride, how we can go places and go for hikes in the woods. She looks at me and smiles.

May 26

Since Mark racked himself up in a Mountain Biking crash, we had a unique opportunity. He is convalescing with me, so I put him to work with Josie. More often than not, Josie is not friendly toward men, most likely because of her early abuse. To start, we had Mark sit in the passenger seat facing out. He is on crutches, so I didn't want him vulnerable to further injury if Josie decided to jump on him. I approached slowly as she does tend to bark and snap at men. She calmly walked up to him and licked his hand.

No hesitation, no fear, nothing! I attribute part of this to Mark's demeanor and the fact that he is a "dog guy." Dogs sense that he is safe. So with the introduction a considerable success, we proceeded to have them both in the RAV4. I opened the back door and gave Josie the "Go for a ride!" command. She would not get in, but this was the rear passenger side, and she never enters from that side. We walked to the driver's side, as soon as I opened the door she jumped right in! This was going perfectly! I closed the door behind her. After I did this, I realized that was a first! Ordinarily, I am in the car with her when I close the door. She gave me a look. Just a brief flash of concern and it was gone from her face. She took her post between the front seats with her paws on the console so she could see what was happening upfront. I put the key in the ignition, and she locked onto it with her eyes. She is so intense as she watches what happens with the key. She startled when I opened the windows, whipping her head around to watch as each one lowered halfway. This was a stronger reaction than when it is just the two of us. She looked first at me then at Mark, anticipating what was coming next. I loved her up until she quieted. She had been panting heavily. Mark asked if that was nervous panting. Since it was a chilly overcast day, it wasn't from the heat. It can be hard to tell them apart, but the tense breathing has an intensity to it. We sat and talked about Josie's behavior and what to expect when I started the engine. We needed to be prepared for anything, and I didn't want to further damage Mark's hip if Josie startled and jumped in his lap. As always, safety first.

With Josie closely watching the key, I started the car. I know I wasn't breathing! But my being anxious would not help the situation, so I relaxed as soon as it was apparent that she wasn't going to panic. The heavy panting resumed, and we both showered her with affection. Once she settled, I turned the car off and made her wait while I got out again. She is told "wait," so she doesn't bolt out of the vehicle. Obviously not wanting her to try to climb over an injured Mark! That would cause him severe pain. Josie waited as commanded; another good sign. If she were in a complete panic, she would not have been able to "wait" another second and would have shoved past me or climbed over my lap, leaving me with claw marks for sure. I'd take that over injuring Mark, but she controlled her impulse, waited as calmly as possible and happily jumped out when I gave her the "OK!" We left the car both relieved and elated!

May 29

My adoration for this dog seems boundless. Today was our first drive! Granted it was only around my property, but it's a start! We started our "walkies" with "go for a ride" as I have been of late. Doing the ride first followed by the walk as a reward seems to have her more enthusiastic about the whole deal. She jumped right into the back seat, the new norm, and I closed the door on her. She once again gave me "the look" that asks if I am leaving her alone in the car. It is so clear on her face that she is terrified that that is what I am doing, but as soon as she sees me open the driver's door, she calms. By calms, I mean she loses the abject fear so evident seconds ago and takes a drink of water. She gets praised and hugged and treated when she calms. I then put the key in the ignition, the laser beam locks on to it as always. The intensity on her face really is something to see! She cocks her head as I start the engine, still not taking her eyes off the ignition.

The panting ensues, and so does more praise, and a few happy "go for a ride!" exclamations. I asked Josie if she was ready to go. She was trembling but not losing it like she had a year ago in the car when she flew into the hatch in abject fear. She stood with her hind feet on the back seat and forepaws on the console, so her head was right next to my shoulder. I put the car in reverse. And slowly backed away. She looked around, and I hugged her head telling her it was OK and that we were going for a ride! I have an acre and a half, so we drove around past the kiln barn, across the driveway and down toward the outdoor kennel we keep for whelping moms, foster dogs, etc., back to the driveway, and after checking in with Josie, around again. I slowly drove back to the front of the house where I park the RAV4 under an old elm tree next to my studio. I wanted Josie to see that we always come back.

After our drive, we took our usual walk, about a mile long, up the road and back. Josie loves her walks and would walk longer if it wasn't so hot. On our return, I took her back to the car to see how she would react. Would Josie refuse to get any closer or would she jump in as usual? I gave her the "easy" command, which keeps her from pulling, and she walked beside me back to the car. I opened the back door, and she jumped right in! Still anxious but did it anyway! This is so amazing to me. That despite her fear, she still gets into the RAV willingly, albeit nervously. I hope that she learns that a ride does not mean she will be left behind. In time it will mean we get to go hiking or to the river but that we will always come home. Always.

June 10

We continue our "rides' around the property though she is still visibly nervous. Curiously she is more worried now just sitting in the running RAV4 than driving in the yard. I have yet to take her down the road, waiting until some of the fear subsides. Though I hope to go for a ride will become something she anticipates with joy and not trepidation. I am starting to wonder if it will. I'd be happy if rides were tolerated without such panic attacks, but only time will tell. For now, her willingness to keep at it despite her fear impresses me no end.

June 14

Well, today was the day! We took our walk this morning before the heat. We walked a little less than a mile and practiced "sit," "down," "leave it" (when we see lizards or snakes.) We have yet to come upon a rattlesnake, but I want Josie to leave any snake

ALONE! Lizards are poisonous to dogs, so I don't want her to eat them. Besides they are good to have around and otherwise harmless. One of the cats ate a lizard, and I found it under my desk chair pretty much whole and coated in regurgitated cat food. Gross, but glad the cat brought it back up!

Josie now has to "sit" and "wait" any time a car goes by. She isn't much of a chaser, but I want her to have a healthy respect for cars. So, we did our walk, and as usual, as we passed the Studio, Josie tried to pull toward the door to go in; a smart girl this one. But I told her we were "going for a ride!" and she followed right along. I opened the RAV door, and in she jumped. I followed, rolled down the windows, started the car, and we drove around the yard as we had been doing. The gate was open, so I thought, "Why not?"

Today was as good a day as any! I turned and headed up the driveway toward the road. Josie was a bit concerned as we passed the gate, we'd never done that before! I could just see on her face what she was thinking. As we headed up the road, Josie was visibly nervous. She had her head by my right shoulder, panting heavily as I rubbed her head and reassured her. She looked out the window to see what was going on and came back next to me. I told her we were going for a ride! Then suddenly she just sat on the back seat. The farther I drove, the calmer she became! It was remarkable! We went just a bit further to a turnaround, and she was back up on my shoulder. "We're going home! Does Josie want to go home?" I asked. Each time we have driven around the yard and pulled back in by the tree, I have told her, "We're Home!" We will always come home. It is so important that she knows that after what she went through. Tomorrow I will see how she is with going for a ride.

June 19

After taking her partway down the road a few days ago, she has been a bit hesitant to get in the car. Before we started actually moving, she would jump into the back seat we are now back to my climbing in first. If I start in, she will follow and leap into the back seat. As long as she is willing to get in, we are continuing the rides.

Today we drove all the way to the end of my road, about 1.5 miles. As before, the longer we drove, the less nervous she became. At one point she even hopped into the back rather than ride facing forward like a sentinel with her front paws on the console. I do hope she will eventually sit in the front seat and not pace back and forth, but each day is a little better. As always time will tell if she ever gets comfortable in a vehicle. I say so far, so good! Today I gave her two cookies when we got back!

June 24

I had some concerns that I had pushed too fast on this. Yesterday Josie didn't want to get in the RAV at all. I sat in the front passenger seat and waited. Eventually, she jumped into the driver's seat but would not venture into the back. Rather than prove myself correct in my concerns, we just sat up front and had treats and lots of attention! I do think that once a ride is followed by a favorite hike, she will come around and relax into the trip knowing her favorite thing, besides treats, is part of the deal.

This has nothing to do with Josie, but it happened yesterday as well. I had received a text last week from our local physician, about a dog that had shown up in Velarde. She was a shepherd mix, young, super sweet, good with the kids, but where did she come from? We exchanged thoughts on scanning for a chip, but the dog left before I could get down there. Yesterday another text came in saying she was back. I was out visiting Violet, who asked to go along as she wanted to meet the Doctor. Since schedules were getting busier as the day went on, we headed right down. Last week I saw the photo of the dog, shepherd/husky for sure. She was a beautiful dog, but nothing out of the ordinary or exceptional. Or so I thought. Violet and I arrived, and as I got out of the car, the dog came directly to me. "Oof!" I felt like I had been kicked in the chest. I turned away with tears in my eyes, needing to breathe and get my bearings. "Oh shit," I said to myself, "What was that?" The dog had not done anything but come over for some attention. Not jumped up, not pushed me, nothing. It was her energy, her very being, that hit me hard. This dog was in every way, just like Blondie. Blondie was not a husky mix, and she wasn't black and cream like this dog either. Their coloring, though both black and tan, was opposite, and their breed mix was different, but their BEING or energy was identical! They were the same size and conformation as well. Once I regained my composure, she pressed up against me, and I loved her all over!! She felt just like Blondie, loved just like Blondie, but without the trauma Blondie suffered her energy was clearer, brighter, but the same. (Blondie had been killed by my neighbors' dogs six months prior.) It was nothing I have ever felt, nor was I prepared for the power of it. It was quite remarkable. She was half Blondie's age, and I do suspect the dogs are half-sisters; same mom with different fathers and from different litters. Had she been a stray, or abandoned, she would have come home with me for sure! We ran the scanner, and she was indeed chipped and spayed at the Espanola Shelter. Her name was Daisy. I spoke with the owner who lived at the end of the street, a dead end. They had cattle and a number of acres, but Daisy liked to visit the Doctor and her children. I suggested the two women get to know each other as Daisy was spending most of her day down the road without the owner's knowledge. It was all good as long as Daisy was safe; every-one was happy to have her around.

July 2

So we are in a bit of a two steps forward one step back situation. After going for a ride for a few days, Josie started to balk at going in the car. The frequency is now back down, and we sit in the RAV as much as we drive around. She isn't any more nervous than before, just more reluctant to get in. While we sit, I have started playing a piece of music, more sound actually, that was designed specifically to calm dogs. In just a few short minutes on Saturday, she jumped in the back and enjoyed the steak snack I had brought. That's the other change; high value treats like leftover steak or beef roll dog treats to reward her for being in the car. But I genuinely do see a difference with the calming sounds. We will prevail, I hope.

July 11

We have been following the above with a little less frequency than previously. A more varied and unpredictable schedule does seem to have Josie less on edge. The calming tunes and having one of the other dogs "Go for a ride" (we aren't yet back to actually moving) has her a bit more at ease. One of the little dogs, Little Fella, an old as dirt Yorkie-Poo that belonged to a friend, who sadly passed away unexpectedly last year, just loves to ride in the car. Or just hang out in it. He scours the floor for any treat left behind then climbs in my lap to help navigate. The other dog that is assisting is Figgie, short for Fig Newton. He too loves the car and is a total love bug. He'll sit in my lap and lick my face until I have no skin left if I let him. Josie watches these two with a look that says, "You like this? Why?" She does seem to comprehend that they are totally comfortable though she may not understand how. Perhaps their comfort will help calm her. The yummy treats aren't hurting either! With time and patience, I think I've used that word before, we will get there. The little dogs who are joining in are really enjoying this. They love to ride in the car, and they get treats too. Josie is excellent with other dogs, and the little ones are fine with her as well. I do hope their enthusiasm rubs off. It certainly can't hurt for her to see that other dogs love being in the RAV. What I struggle with is how deeply afraid Josie is even after all this time. And perhaps it only seems like a long time to me! To Josie it might feel like just yesterday she was dumped. Since dogs do not share our sense of time, this is entirely possible. Having trapped her and trucked her here, she just may need more time to trust that this is good. So we once again keep calm and carry on.

Josie is a tough case. Her trauma is deep. She is the only dog in my care that is afraid of thunder storms so she tends to be high strung. Pile on abuse and abandonment and we have our work cut put for us! All-in-all she is a smart, sweet dog but she is choosy about her human and dog companions. She is on our website as well as www.FindingRover.com

The Story of Bonnie and Clyde
by Bonnie Parker

You've read the story of Jesse James
Of how he lived and died;
If you're still in need
Of something to read,
Here's the story of Bonnie and Clyde.

This is the story of Bonnie and Clyde. Not enough of a story for a full chapter. It is more of the day-to-day variety.

Today is May 13th, 2019. We are in the middle of another beautiful adoption, but it wasn't without its problems. Almost two weeks ago two cute, sweet hound mix puppies were dumped at the end of the Cañoncito road. In the same place, Baby Girl was dropped last year. It is a conjunction of Dixon and the Ojo Sarco, Truchas, Trampas area. As people drive down from the mountains, this is where residences reappear after miles of Federal land. People who abandon their pups know either the puppies will be eaten by coyote or mountain lion or someone will care for them if found. They lucked out when they chose to hang out at the Atencio's. These two hounds had huge feet and would be large dogs. They were approximately three months old and bonded to one another. They were so sweet to watch as they curled up in their dog house at their foster home. I named them Bonnie and Clyde as the foster family owns a husky named Capone. We just carried the gangster theme forward. We scanned them for chips though none were expected. We weren't wrong about that. We posted them as found, no one claimed them. We posted them as available and that we wanted to keep them together if possible. The foster family loved them, but they already had four dogs. Another two were out of the question.

We were entering a week of bad weather. We generally don't see long periods of rain like we were going to see that week. This meant we needed to weatherize the kennel with tarps and warm blankets.

I was there every day for three days helping get them set with food and shelter. In the evening on Wednesday, the foster mom called to say that Clyde wouldn't come out of the dog house and hadn't eaten all day. Too often dumped puppies will have been exposed to Parvovirus. If Clyde had Parvo Bonnie would most likely break with it in a day or two, and I had inadvertently exposed my tiny six-pound pup to it as well. Not good. I went to check on Clyde and immediately called to see if Cottonwood could take him; they were full. I called Taos to see which Vet was on emergency call that night. It was Dr. Kim at Salazar Vet Clinic, one of the best around, and I was grateful!

I rushed him in and gave her the rundown. Appears to be Parvo but without vomiting and diarrhea. Not all that unusual as it can affect every dog differently. We ran a Parvo test, it was negative. We may have caught it so early that he wasn't shedding the virus yet, and by his symptoms, she still suspected Parvo. Rather than leave him at the clinic, she asked me to treat him at home. OK. Not ideal, but it would work. I bundled Clyde, his blankets, and a bag full of fluids and antibiotics into the car and headed back. At least at home, he'd have his Bonnie to snuggle and keep him warm. He was good with treatment for the night. Now safely in the dog house with Bonnie resting her head on his back, it was time for all of us to get some sleep. In the morning, he seemed a bit better and was a stellar patient as I administered the antibiotic injection, anti-nausea meds, and more fluids. Bonnie stayed curled up with him through-out. We knew it would be up and down for a few days but so far, so good! That evening, after a day of cold rain, I headed back over for Clyde's evening treatment. When I approached the dog house, I could see that Clyde wasn't moving and I was sure he was dead. I crawled into the dog house, screaming, "NOOOO!" He was such a sweet soul, he needed to get better for Bonnie, for all of us! What is Bonnie without her Clyde?? I had to control my emotions; I didn't want to upset the foster family. It was going to be hard enough. I sat stroking a motionless Clyde telling him how he was loved when he picked his head up and groaned. "Oh, Clyde!" I cried as I bundled him in my arms to rush him back into the emergency vet. This time his temperature was a little low where previously it was a bit high. That was unusual for Parvo. In the car, I had placed him in a crate, and he had a bout of diarrhea, but it was not characteristic of Parvo either. Parvo produces bloody diarrhea; this was not. Still, if we were in the early stages who knows? My car stank something awful, but I didn't care. The mess was contained, and Clyde was still fighting. We set him up in the isolation ward with warm fluids. He would be safe and snug for the night. As I prepared to go home, he tried to get up. At first, he sat up; we thought he might need to vomit, he didn't. He was trying to stand, but he was so weak he couldn't support himself and sat back down. I stroked him and gave him kisses and asked him to please keep fighting. We agreed that I would call in the morning for an update. At that point, we would decide if he came home or stayed another night in the hospital. In the morning when I called, I was put on hold so they could find a Doctor. I knew then that he had died. That was confirmed. We had done all that we could; it wasn't enough. We would never know what had killed him.

Clyde was tiny compared to Bonnie and too thin. He may have had a congenital issue that just broke loose. He may have eaten something poisonous, or it could have been Parvo even though the test was negative. We just don't know. I hung up and hung my head to cry. Clyde was one of those souls that just grabs your heart and gives it a big squeeze. Such a beautiful, sweet dog that didn't deserve what he got. Poor Bonnie was depressed without her Clyde. We all cried both for ourselves and for sweet Bonnie. If she was exposed to Parvo, we would have to wait a week before we could adopt her out. We wanted to be sure she didn't get sick. I had the meds ready if she should break with it. She didn't. Neither did my little pup. As of this writing, we are not totally out of the woods yet, but we are through the peak incubation period. So we waited. The day after Clyde died, the foster mom texted me to ask if they could adopt her. More tears!! This time of joy. This is a wonderful family who takes such good care of their dogs! If the other dogs were accepting of Bonnie, it was a done deal! I'm still waiting to see how that is going, but paws crossed that they will get along.

I checked in a few weeks later. Bonnie had grown! Almost doubled in size and was playing happily with Capone and another older dog. She was getting all of her immunizations, and she never showed any signs of illness. Bonnie was one lucky dog.

Like Josie, Ginny has many issues to be overcome or at least diminished as much as possible. Our Daily training walks continue and as she moves into young adulthood she is calming, a little.

In all dog training consistency is critical. So on walk #2, when Mark had Ginny, and she pulled him all over the yard, she received mixed signals. I had Josie at a safe distance. The girls were on their first walk together. We switched dogs so I could keep the "tree" going with Ginny. I reminded Mark that Josie wasn't allowed to pull either! Josie is much better now after I switched her off an extendable leash to a 6 footer. I had a reason for starting her training on an extendable, something I don't generally recommend, but right now it escapes me! All I can come up with is that I wanted to work on recall, so she needed to be able to go a distance away. I don't generally recommend extendable leashes because it is too easy for a dog who is not good at recall (also known as "come") to end up on the other side of the road when a car is coming. The leash is relatively narrow so easy for a driver to miss. I've heard horror stories of dogs getting killed this way. The owner always blames the retractible! I'm afraid I can't agree with that. In an area with little or no traffic they can be useful in training but not a good idea for general walking.

The other method I use is a training exercise to keep the dog more focused on the walker. It is a game we play both in the kennel and on the leash. I've heard it called "Tornado" or "Roundabout." It is merely a treat tossing game. But it gets a dog's attention!

To play, you show the dog a treat and turn them 180 around you and toss it for them to fetch. The dog will undoubtedly come back for more! Repeat until you or the dog are too dizzy to continue! If you do it daily, you do build a tolerance for the spinning motion. As a figure skater, it's pretty much a non-issue as we spin all the time. I just have to be sure I rotate in my natural direction, counter-clockwise. Believe it or not, dogs also have a dominant or natural direction. Lucky for me, Ginny shares my rotation. I tried the turn in each direction.

She was enthusiastic about going one way but would not turn clockwise! Since I had Mark as a willing participant, the last two walks were with both Josie and Ginny. They were so distracted by the other during those walks that I took them out separately today. Buddy joined us on both treks. Both dogs are great with Buddy, but I see some lip- licking from Josie that has me cautious about letting her be too close to Ginny just yet. They have met and showed some posturing but nothing outwardly aggressive, yet. I'd like to keep it that way! I do think eventually they can be allowed more contact. Today I wanted to focus on Ginny and reducing the pulling. By the time we headed back, we walk about a mile total, she would stop and turn as soon as she felt the pull on the leash. As we approached the house, she was walking on a loose leash without correction. I am pleased. She spent half her life on a chain, often trying to pull free, so I'd say she's doing well!

She's been on a few walks since last week and is really settling into the routine. She will sit or stand calmly as I put on her harness. We are on harness number three now. The first was an older harness donated by a local dog owner whose dog passed away. It is a beautiful harness, but Ginny is so active that I'm afraid she'll just break out of it. Harness number two was a Premiere Easy Walk, one of my favorite harnesses for pullers. I grabbed Josie's EW and headed out. It worked great as always until we returned home, and Ginny was reluctant to go back to her kennel. She preferred to play with Buddy!

Though it was great that Ginny wanted to play, as she may never have had the chance to play with another dog. She didn't really understand how to play yet. In her exuberance, this pittie girl was pretty much out of her harness! She'd pulled right out! I have never had a dog that could pull out like that, with such ease. I was a bit concerned and would need to go shopping for a different style of harness. Like most pit bulls, she is broad-chested, thick of neck, almost as big around as her head, so she was nearly a wedge. This shape makes it harder to get a good fit on any harness. In the meantime, she honestly did not want to go back in the kennel, but I needed to re-harness her and tighten her collar so she couldn't run free, and I needed to do it fast! I picked her up and carried her to the kennel so I could safely adjust both. I had left her collar loose so she could get used to wearing it without it annoying her. She didn't seem to mind a collar at all, but I had neglected to properly tighten it before taking her out. This could have been a disaster; it was quickly averted.

I knew I'd dodged a serious bullet, this time.

I need Mark or another body to walk Josie if we are all going together. Mark hasn't been available, so the two girls have been getting separate walks with Buddy, lucky guy. All has been going really well with both girls learning not to pull, even when something smells interesting. Then it snowed. That was last Monday. Mark had a meeting in Santa Fe, so I was on my own. On Mondays, I am more tired than usual after a long day of teaching or in this case, the day after the Super Bowl. I am a Patriots fan. To those who hate the Pats, I am sorry, but I grew up in a Boston suburb. When I was in advertising in the 1980s, the Patriots were a client at the Agency I worked for. That was great fun. Growing up, I loved football. Watching it or playing it, I loved it and still do. This Super Bowl was a tense game, lowest scoring in Super Bowl history. Both teams had such strong defense it remained scoreless for two quarters. OK, I'm getting off track.

Our day-to-day routine remains fairly constant. Ginny walks beautifully as long as her other pal Kayne isn't chewing on her leg or neck. Kayne is a young pit mix, and they adore each other. It's wonderful unless we're trying to walk! Cars are still a problem as Ginny wants to chase them, just like Buddy and Kayne do, but the boys are off leash. Working again that isn't easy. She no longer chases lizards; that's big!

Ginny is on our website www.DAPSNM.org and Finding Rover. com. We hope the perfect adopter finds her soon.

$15.00
ISBN 978-1-7341032-0-5

51500>